Ninja Foodi Grill Cookbook 2021

1000-Days Easy & Delicious Indoor Grilling and Air Frying Recipes

for Beginners and Advanced Users

Cheryl Benjamin

© Copyright 2021 - All rights reserved

This document is geared towards providing exact and reliable information with regards to the topic and issue covered. The publication is sold with the idea that the publisher is not required to render accounting, officially permitted, or otherwise, qualified services. If advice is necessary, legal, or professional, a practiced individual in the profession should be ordered. - From a Declaration of Principles which was accepted and approved equally by a Committee of the American Bar Association and a Committee of Publishers and Associations. In no way is it legal to reproduce, duplicate, or transmit any part of this document in either electronic means or in printed format. Recording of this publication is strictly prohibited and any storage of this document is not allowed unless with written permission from the publisher.

All rights reserved. The information provided herein is stated to be truthful and consistent, in that any liability, in terms of inattention or otherwise, by any usage or abuse of any policies, processes, or directions contained within is the solitary and utter responsibility of the recipient reader.

Under no circumstances will any legal responsibility or blame be held against the publisher for any reparation, damages, or monetary loss due to the information herein, either directly or indirectly. Respective authors own all copyrights not held by the publisher.

The information herein is offered for informational purposes solely, and is universal as so. The presentation of the information is without contract or any type of guarantee assurance. The trademarks that are used are without any consent, and the publication of the trademark is without permission or backing by the trademark owner.

All trademarks and brands within this book are for clarifying purposes only and are the owned by the owners themselves, not affiliated with this document.

Table of Contents

Introduction **5**

About Ninja Foodi Grill **6**

   Functions and Buttons 6

   Features of The Ninja Foodi Grill 7

   Cleaning Your Ninja Foodi Grill 7

   Benefits of Ninja Foodi Grill 7

Breakfast **8**

   Spinach Omelet 9

   Breakfast Hash 10

   Mushroom and Black Olives Omelet ... 11

   Spinach and Cheese Muffins 12

   Regular Grilled Cheese Bread 13

   Breakfast Soufflé 14

   Sourdough Sandwich 15

   Air Fry Sweet Potatoes 16

Poultry Mains **17**

   Grilled Chicken 18

   Ninja Foodi Grill Savory Chicken Breast 19

   Chicken with Tzatziki Sauce 20

   Cheesy Chicken Wings 21

   Honey Garlic Chicken Wings 22

   Air Crisp Drumstick 23

   Crispy Chicken 24

   Orange and Honey Glazed Chicken 25

   Alfredo Apple Chicken 26

   BBQ Chicken Thighs 27

   Grilled BBQ Chicken 28

   Yogurt Chicken Thighs 29

   Chicken Beans and Chili 30

   Chicken Tomatina 31

Snacks and Appetizers **32**

   Snack Time Pizza 33

   Air Crisp Chicken Tenders 34

   Spicy Chicken Tenders 35

   Grilled Watermelon 36

   French Fries with Parmesan 37

   Maple and Rosemary Chicken Wing 38

   Kale Chips 39

   Stuffed Bell Peppers 40

   Cinnamon Butternut Squash 41

   Stuffed Mushrooms 42

   Fried Broccoli 43

Vegetables and Sides **44**

   Sweet Potato Fingers 45

   Mexican Street Corn 46

   Honey & Herb Charred Carrots 47

   Roasted Cauliflower 48

Grilled Tomato Salsa 49

Eggplant with Greek yogurt 50

Stuffed Jalapeno 51

Parmesan, Cheddar, And Zucchini Casserole 52

Artichokes with Honey Dijon 53

Garlic and Sage Tomatoes 54

Fish and Seafood............................ 55

Teriyaki Salmon 56

Grilled Citrusy Halibut 57

Salmon with Herbs 58

Lemon Pepper Shrimp 59

Glazed Salmon 60

Smoked Shrimp 61

Salmon with Creamy Lime Sauce 62

Salmon with Cream Cheese 63

Sea Food Omelet 64

Shrimp Poppers 65

Pineapple Fish Fillet 66

Coconut Battered Fish Fillets 67

Beef, Pork, And Lamb...................... 68

Ninja Foodi Grill Steak and Potatoes ... 69

Ninja Foodi Grill Steak 70

Grilled Steak 71

Soy Pork Ribs 72

Lamb Chops 73

Air Fry Ground Beef 74

Beef Jerky 75

Pork Chops 76

Sausages in Ninja Grill 77

Greek Yogurt Lamb Chops 78

Steak & Vegetable Kebabs 79

Lamb Chops with Coconut 80

Rosemary Lamb Chops 81

Best Pork Chops 82

Dessert 83

Banana and Chocolate Chip Pudding ... 84

Lava Cake 85

Delicious Pie 86

Chocolate Chip Cake 87

Blueberry Muffins 88

Bread Pudding 89

Vanilla Cake 90

Grilled Pineapple 91

Grilled Cinnamon Apple 92

Grilled Bananas 93

30 Days Meal Plan 94

Conclusion 96

Introduction

Versatile, yummy, and grilled food is what the Ninja Foodi grill cookbook is all about. The Ninja Foodi grill is a new way to enjoy grill food indoor, which is prepared straight in the kitchen and served to your dining tables.

If you love the grill and perfectly chard food that is unique, delicious, and easy to prepare then the Ninja Foodi grill offers a quick-cooking style and makes every meal a special treat and gives a fresh vibe to the food.

This cookbook covers some astonishing recipes that are prepared using Ninja Foodi grill using some of the best whole, hearty, and healthy ingredients. All the recipes are created by adding some extra twist to them.

Before getting toward the recipe part, it is very important to get to know about the grill, its functions, and tip and trick to maintain and use the appliance.

The meals that are introduced in this book are targeted towards all the family members, includes everything from breakfast, lunch, snacks, dessert, to mouthwatering dinners.

We are covering the following:

- Introduction about the Ninja grill
- Useful Buttons and Function
- Benefits of Using Ninja Grill
- Tips and Cautions of Usage
- 80 mouthwatering recipes
- Meal plan
- Conclusion

Now, let's get started.

About Ninja Foodi Grill

Ninja Foodi grill is the best way to prepare sizzling, chard, and grilled food items indoor with ease. It is an indoor appliance that can cook smartly using its precooked functions of the grill, roast, and air crisp, dehydrate and bake. The ninja Foodi grill comes with its grill grate, crisper basket, and grill brush. It offers a 90-day money-back guarantee, along with a complete guide to follow.

The ninja Foodi grill smart function allows you to cook food smartly with a smart thermometer that helps to achieve perfect doneness from rare to well done.

It circulates hot air around the food that makes the food cook with a perfect sear and chard grill marks and flavor that is cooked using a cyclonic technology, that brings the outdoor grill flavor to the food the ninja Foodi grill.

It can air crisp the food with 70 % less oil, than the traditional way of cooking.

Functions and Buttons

- GRILL: the grill button helps to cook perfect chard grilled food.
- AIR CRISP: this function is used to prepare mouthwatering, light, low fat, and crispy meals.
- BAKE: help to bake biscuits, muffins, cakes, desserts, and other items.

- ROAST: Roast meat and veggies to their tender perfection.
- DEHYDRATE: it is used to dehydrate food items.

Features of The Ninja Foodi Grill

- Cyclonic Grilling Technology
- Dimensions: 17 L x 14 W x 11 H
- Weight: 14.5 pounds
- 500F Degree Cyclonic Air
- Wattage: 1760 watts
- Material: Stainless steel
- Functions: Grill, roast, the air crisp, and dehydrate
- Nonstick ceramic-coated removable parts
- Capacity: 10" x 10" grill grate
- 4-qt crisper basket
- a 6-qt cooking pot
- Dishwasher Safe accessories
- 1-year warranty

Cleaning Your Ninja Foodi Grill

- Before cleaning the ninja Foodi grill unplug and let the unit cool off.
- Take out the crisper basket, grill grate, and cooking pans along with a brush, and then wash it in the dishwasher, for easy and safe cleaning.
- Use a damp cloth to clean the outer surface of the unit and then dry with a paper towel.
- It is not recommended to immerse the unit in water
- The thermometer is not dishwasher safe and you need to clean it manually.

Benefits of Ninja Foodi Grill

- It provides an odor-free cooking experience
- It can cook food with a very low-fat content
- It provides a hand-free cooking experience
- The cleaning and maintenance are very easy
- Multifunctional appliance allowing the function of the oven, dehydrator, and outdoor grill
- One-touch technology makes it easy to operate

Breakfast

Spinach Omelet

Prep: 10 Minutes | Cook Time: 6 Minutes | Makes: 2 Servings

Ingredients

- 2 eggs, whisked
- 2 tablespoons of full-fat milk
- ¼ cup of baby spinach, chopped
- ½ cup of shredded cheese
- Salt and pepper, to taste
- Oil spray, for greasing
- 4 cherry tomatoes, halved

Directions

1. Take A Bowl and Crack Eggs in It Along with Milk.
2. Whisk Both the Ingredients.
3. Then Add Spinach and Cherry Tomatoes.
4. Give It A Whisk and Season It with Salt and Black Pepper.
5. At the End Add A Handful of Cheese.
6. Take A Veggies Tray and Grease It with Oil Spray.
7. Place the Veggie Tray Inside the Ninja Grill Crisper Tray in The Ninja Foodi Grill to Start the Preheating For 10 Minutes At 350 Degrees F.
8. Once Preheating Is Done Add the Veggies Tray Inside the Unit and AIR CRISP for 6 Minutes At 360 Degrees F.
9. Once Done Sprinkle Some Additional Cheese If Desired.
10. Enjoy the Omelet as A Healthy Breakfast.

Serving Suggestion: Serve with toast

Variation Tip: Use almond milk instead of full-fat dairy milk

Nutritional Information per Serving: Calories 234| Fat 15g | Sodium 260mg | Carbs 11.2g | Fiber3 g| Sugar7.7 g | Protein 15.4g

Breakfast Hash

Prep: 15 Minutes | Cook Time: 12 Minutes | Makes: 3 Servings

Ingredients

- 2 cups of potatoes, shredded
- 4 tablespoons of chive, chopped
- 1 cup of parmesan cheese
- ½ cup cheddar cheese
- ¼ cup of canola oil
- Salt and black pepper, as desired
- 2 eggs, beaten
- ½ teaspoon of onion powder
- ½ tsp of garlic powder

Directions

1. Sprinkle salt over the shredded potatoes and set aside for 20 minutes.
2. Squeeze the shredded potatoes to drain excess liquid.
3. Take a bowl and whisk eggs in it.
4. Then add chives, salt, pepper, onion powder, and garlic powder
5. Mix it all very well.
6. Then add shredded cheeses and potato.
7. Take a cooking pot and place it into the Ninja Foodi Grill.
8. And close the grill hood and preheat the unit to 350 degrees F or 10 minutes
9. Afterward, grease a cooking pot with oil spray and add the egg mixture to the pot.
10. Place it inside the ninja Foodi grill and close the hood.
11. Let it AIR CRISP at 350 degrees F for 12 minutes.
12. Once done, take out and serve.

Serving Suggestion: serve it with ketchup

Variation Tip: use garlic cloves instead of garlic powered

Nutritional Information per Serving: Calories 532 | Fat 40g | Sodium 684mg | Carbs 19g | Fiber 2.6g| Sugar 1.8 g | Protein 2

Mushroom and Black Olives Omelet

Prep: 10 Minutes | Cook Time: 8 Minutes | Makes: 3 Servings

Ingredients

- 5 eggs, whisked
- 4 tablespoons of cheddar cheese
- ¼ cup of mushrooms, chopped
- 2 tablespoons of black olives, chopped
- Salt and black pepper, to taste
- Oil spray, for greasing

Directions

1. Take a bowl, and crack eggs in it.
2. Whisk it well and add cheddar cheese.
3. Then add mushrooms, black olives.
4. Give it a whisk and season it with salt and black pepper.
5. Take a round aluminum pan and place it inside the Ninja grill crisper basket to start the preheating at 350 degrees F for 10 minutes.
6. Once preheating is done, pour the egg in the round pan and AIRCRISP for 8 minutes at 360 degrees F.
7. Enjoy the omelet as a healthy breakfast.

Serving Suggestion: serve it with ketchup

Variation Tip: Use green olives instead of black

Nutritional Information per Serving: Calories152 | Fat 11.2g | Sodium210 mg | Carbs1.2 g | Fiber 0.3g| Sugar 0.7g | Protein 12g

Spinach and Cheese Muffins

Prep: 15 Minutes | Cook Time: 20 Minutes | Makes: 4 Servings

Ingredients

- 4 strips of veggies breakfast bacon, chopped
- ½ large onion, chopped
- ½ cups cheddar cheese, shredded
- ½ cup of spinach
- 4 organic large eggs
- Salt and black pepper, to taste

Directions

1. Take a skillet and add a bacon strip to it.
2. Let it cook for 2 minutes then add onions.
3. Let the onion get tender.
4. Then add spinach and let the spinach cook for 2 minutes.
5. Remove it from the skillet and let the mixture cool down, completely.
6. Then whisk the egg in a bowl and season it with salt and black pepper.
7. Add spinach mixture to the egg as well and stir all the ingredients.
8. Pour this mixture amongst ramekins.
9. Arrange the ramekins into the preheated Ninja Foodi Grill.
10. Press the Bake button and set the temperature to 350°F.
11. Adjust the time to 20 minutes, and close the hood, and let it bake.
12. Once done, serve and enjoy with cheddar cheese topping.

Serving Suggestion: Serve it with toast

Variation Tip: Use parmesan cheese instead of cheddar cheese

Nutritional Information per Serving: Calories 197| Fat14.2 g | Sodium381 mg | Carbs4.5 g | Fiber 1.5g| Sugar 1.3g | Protein 12.1g

Regular Grilled Cheese Bread

Prep: 12 Minutes | Cook Time: 8 Minutes | Makes: 1 Serving

Ingredients
- 2 slices of Italian bread
- 1 slice of parmesan cheese
- 1 slice of cheddar cheese
- 2 tablespoons of butter

Directions
1. Take the bread slices and coat both bread on one side with butter.
2. Then put slices of both the cheese on one slice and top it with the other slice.
3. Press the Bake button of the ninja Foodi grill and set the temperature of 350°F for 5 minutes
4. Press start to begin preheating.
5. Once preheating is done, put the sandwich in the ninja Foodi grill grate.
6. Adjust the time to 8 minutes, and close the hood, and let it bake.
7. Once 4 minutes pass, open the hood and flip the bread slice to cook from the other side.
8. Once it's done serve.

Serving Suggestion: Serve it with coffee

Variation Tip: Use a slice of your favorite cheeses.

Nutritional Information per Serving: Calories 275| Fat 22.5g | Sodium 487mg | Carbs 6.2g | Fiber0.3 g| Sugar0.2 g | Protein 13.5g

Breakfast Soufflé

Prep: 10 Minutes | Cook Time: 10 Minutes | Makes: 2 Servings

Ingredients

- 4 eggs, beaten
- 2 teaspoons of coconut cream
- 2tablespoons of heavy cream
- ½ teaspoon of red chili flakes
- 2 tablespoons of chives, chopped
- Salt and black pepper, to taste

Directions

1. Take a cooking pot and place it inside the ninja Foodi grill.
2. Close the hood and preheat the unit at bake function for 10 minutes at 350 degrees F.
3. Take a large bowl and crack eggs in it.
4. Whisk the eggs and add salt, pepper, chives, red chili flakes, heavy cream, coconut cream, and whisk it all well.
5. Pour this mixture equally amongst oil greased soufflé dishes.
6. Put the dishes inside the cooking pot of the Ninja Foodi Grill and close the hood.
7. Let it bake for 10 minutes at 350 degrees F.
8. Once done, serve.

Serving Suggestion: Serve with bagels

Variation Tip: Use parsley instead of chives

Nutritional Information per Serving: Calories190 | Fat 15.5g | Sodium 130mg | Carbs1.5 g | Fiber 0.2g| Sugar 0.9g | Protein 11.6g

Sourdough Sandwich

Prep: 10 Minutes | Cook Time: 7 Minutes | Makes: 2 Servings

Ingredients

- 4 sourdough bread slices
- 3 tablespoons softened butter
- 2 sharp Cheddar cheese slices
- 2 ounces of Havarti cheese slices

Directions

1. Insert the grill grate inside the unit.
2. Preheat the ninja Foodi grill to 375 degrees F, for 5 minutes.
3. Meanwhile spread the butter on all four slices of bread.
4. Place two slices butter side down inside the ninja Foodi grill grate.
5. Top each bread piece with 1 slice of Cheddar and 1 slice of Havarti.
6. Put the remaining bread slices on top, buttered side up.
7. "AIR CRISP" it for 7 minutes at a360 degrees F.
8. Once 3 minutes pass, open the hood and flip the bread slice to cook from the other side.
9. Once done, serve.

Serving Suggestion: Serve with milk tea

Variation Tip: Use parmesan cheese instead of Havarti cheese

Nutritional Information per Serving: Calories408| Fat 36.7g | Sodium 883mg | Carbs 38g | Fiber 1.5g| Sugar2.8 g | Protein21.7 g

Air Fry Sweet Potatoes

Prep: 10 Minutes | Cook Time: 10 Minutes | Makes: 1 Serving

Ingredients

- 1 sweet potato peeled and cubed
- 1 teaspoon olive oil
- 1/2 teaspoon kosher salt
- 1/4 teaspoon black pepper fresh cracked
- 1/2 teaspoon smoked paprika

Directions

1. Preheat the ninja Foodi grill by setting it to 400 degrees F for 5 minutes.
2. Take a large bowl and add potatoes along with oil and all the listed slices.
3. Toss it well for fine coating.
4. Grease the cooking pot of the ninja Foodi grill.
5. Transfer the cubes of potatoes to the cooking pot inside the ninja Foodi grill.
6. Set it to AIRCRISP mode at 400 F for 10 minutes.
7. Once done, serve.

Serving Suggestion: Serve with ketchup

Variation Tip: Use canola oil instead of olive oil

Nutritional Information per Serving: Calories 143| Fat 4.8g | Sodium 1233mg | Carbs 23.6g | Fiber4.4 g| Sugar 7.1g | Protein2.2 g

Poultry Mains

Grilled Chicken

Prep: 15 Minutes | Cook Time: 27 Minutes | Makes: 4 Servings

Ingredients

- 4 chicken breasts, frozen boneless, skinless (8 ounces each)
- 3 tablespoons canola oil
- Salt and black pepper, to taste
- 1 cup of barbecue sauce

Directions

1. First, insert the grill grate in the ninja food grill and select the grill function.
2. Set the time to 25 minutes at medium.
3. Select start to begin preheating.
4. Meanwhile brush the chicken with oil, salt, and black pepper.
5. Once preheating is done, place chicken breasts on the grill grate.
6. Close the unit hood and cook for 10 minutes.
7. After 10 minutes, flip the chicken to cook from the other side
8. Close the hood and let it cook for 5 minutes.
9. After 5 minutes open the hood and baste the chicken with barbecue sauce, and give it a final flip
10. Close hood and cook for 7 or more minutes until internal temperate reaches 165 degrees F.
11. Serve and enjoy after letting the chicken rest for 5 minutes.

Serving Suggestion: Serve with coleslaw

Variation Tip: Use vegetable oil instead of canola oil

Nutritional Information per Serving: Calories618 | Fat 27.5g | Sodium894 mg | Carbs 22.7g | Fiber0.4 g| Sugar16.3 g | Protein 65.6g

Ninja Foodi Grill Savory Chicken Breast

Prep: 15 Minutes | Cook Time: 22 Minutes | Makes: 4 Servings

Ingredients

- 4 Chicken Breasts
- 1/2 Cup Olive Oil
- 4 tablespoons Soy Sauce
- 2 tablespoons Balsamic Vinegar
- 1/3 Cup Brown Sugar
- ½ tablespoon of garlic powder
- 1 teaspoon for onion powder
- Salt & pepper to taste

Directions

1. Take a bowl and mix all the listed ingredients, excluding chicken breast pieces.
2. Whisk, all the ingredients very well to make a marinade.
3. Poke the chicken breasts with a fork and add to the marinade.
4. Let the chicken marinate for 30 minutes.
5. First, insert the grill grate in the ninja food grill and select the grill function.
6. Set the time to 25 minutes at medium.
7. Select start to begin preheating.
8. Once preheating completes, add the chicken breasts onto grill grates, close the hood, and set it to 10 minutes.
9. Afterward, open the hood and flip the breast pieces and baste the chicken with marinade.
10. Cook for another 12 minutes.
11. Once the internal temperate reaches 165 degrees F, it's done.
12. Baste the chicken one more time and serve and enjoy after letting the chicken rest for 5 minutes.

Serving Suggestion: Serve with ranch

Variation Tip: use coconut amino instead of soy sauce

Nutritional Information per Serving: Calories556 | Fat36.1 g | Sodium 1036mg | Carbs 14.7g | Fiber 0.4g| Sugar 12.5g | Protein 43.6g

Chicken with Tzatziki Sauce

Prep: 15 Minutes | Cook Time: 20 Minutes | Makes: 4 Servings

Ingredients

For the Grilled Chicken Breasts:

- 4-6 chicken breasts pieces, skinless
- 2 tablespoons extra-virgin olive oil
- 1 tablespoon oregano, dry
- ½ tablespoon garlic powder
- 1 lemon, juice only
- salt and freshly grounded pepper to taste

For the Tzatziki Sauce:

- ½ cup cucumber, grated and unpeeled
- 1 cup of Greek yogurt
- 1 tablespoon of apple cider vinegar
- 1 lemon, juice only
- 1 tablespoon of garlic powder

Directions

1. Take a bowl and mix lemon juice, olive oil, salt, pepper, garlic, and oregano.
2. Marinate chicken in it for 1 hour inside the refrigerator.
3. Squeeze the cucumber liquid and add it to a large bowl.
4. Add the remaining listed ingredients under tzatziki sauce and mix well
5. Set it aside for further use.
6. Preheat the Ninja Foodi grill to 400 degrees at MAX.
7. Select start to begin preheating.
8. Afterward, add chicken onto the grill grate, and cook the chicken breasts for about 10 minutes per side.
9. Once done, remove it from the grill.
10. Serve with prepared sauce.

Serving Suggestion: Serve with baked potato

Variation Tip: Use lime instead of lemon juice

Nutritional Information per Serving: Calories 1239| Fat59 g | Sodium 500mg | Carbs27.2 g | Fiber1 g| Sugar 25g | Protein 145g

Cheesy Chicken Wings

Prep: 15 Minutes | Cook Time: 15 Minutes | Makes: 3 Servings

Ingredients

- 12 Chicken wings
- 2 teaspoons of olive oil
- Salt and pepper
- 1/4 cup butter
- 1 teaspoon of garlic powder
- 1/3 cup parmesan cheese, grated
- 1/3 teaspoon Italian seasoning, dried
- ½ tablespoon lemon juice

Directions

1. First, insert the grill grate in the ninja food grill and select the grill function.
2. Set the time to 25mintues at medium.
3. Select start to begin preheating.
4. Take a bowl and add wings to it.
5. Then season the wings with salt and black pepper.
6. Then add oil and coat the wings evenly with it.
7. Next add butter garlic powder, Italian seasoning, and lemon juice.
8. Afterward, add chicken inside the ninja Foodi grill and grill at high for 15 minutes.
9. Remember to flip halfway through.
10. Once done sprinkle parmesan cheese on top.
11. Enjoy hot.

Serving Suggestion: Serve it with baked potatoes

Variation Tip: Use lime juice instead of lemon juice

Nutritional Information per Serving: Calories 881| Fat66.6 g | Sodium 962mg | Carbs 23.1g | Fiber 0.7g| Sugar 0.3g | Protein47.1 g

Honey Garlic Chicken Wings

Prep: Minutes | Cook Time: 35 Minutes | Makes: 2 Servings

Ingredients

- 8 chicken wings
- ¼ cup flour
- Salt & pepper to taste
- 2 tablespoons olive oil

Sauce Ingredients

- ¼ cup honey
- 3 tablespoons soy sauce
- 2 large garlic cloves crushed
- 1 tablespoon ginger finely diced
- ¼ teaspoon chili flakes
- 1 teaspoon corn starch
- ¼ cup water

Directions

1. Take a bowl and whisk together all the sauce ingredients.
2. Set it aside for further use.
3. First, insert the crisper basket in the ninja food grill and select the AIR CRIPS function
4. Set the time to 25 minutes at the medium.
5. Select start to begin preheating.
6. Rub the wings with olive oil, salt, and pepper and dust them with flour.
7. Afterward, add chicken inside the ninja Foodi grill and AIRCRISP for 35 minutes at 390 degrees F.
8. Remember to flip halfway through.
9. Once done take it out and dump it in sauce and finely coat it all over serve hot.

Serving Suggestion: Serve with salad

Variation Tip: Use canola oil instead of olive oil

Nutritional Information per Serving: Calories1271 | Fat 78.3g | Sodium 2297mg | Carbs80.9 g | Fiber1.6 g| Sugar 35.2g | Protein 61.2g

Air Crisp Drumstick

Prep: 12 Minutes | Cook Time: 25 Minutes | Makes: 2 Servings

Ingredients
- 8 chicken drumsticks
- 4 teaspoons olive oil
- Salt and black pepper, to taste
- 1 tablespoon garlic powder
- 1 teaspoon of smoked paprika
- 1/2 teaspoon of cumin
- 1/2 teaspoon of thyme

Directions
1. Take a medium bowl and mix all the listed herbs and spices.
2. Add in the drumsticks and drizzle with olive oil.
3. Finely coat the chicken pieces and then marinate them for 30 minutes.
4. First, insert the grill grate in the ninja food grill and select the grill function.
5. Set the time to 25 minutes at medium.
6. Select start to begin preheating.
7. Once preheating is done add chicken pieces to the unit.
8. Grill it at high for 25 minutes.
9. Remember to flip it halfway through.
10. Once done, take out and serve.

Serving Suggestion: Serve with Mac and cheese

Variation Tip: Use canola oil instead of olive oil

Nutritional Information per Serving: Calories410 | Fat20.1 g | Sodium 150mg | Carbs 4g | Fiber0.9 g| Sugar1.1 g | Protein51.6 g

Crispy Chicken

Prep: 15 Minutes | Cook Time: 24 Minutes | Makes: 2 Servings

Ingredients

- ½ cup of coconut amino
- ¼ cup balsamic vinegar
- 2 garlic cloves, minced
- 2 tablespoons cornstarch
- 2 tablespoons cold water
- ½ cup white sugar
- 1 teaspoon ground pepper
- 1 teaspoon ground ginger
- 10 chicken thighs
- Salt and black pepper, to taste

Directions

1. In a mixing bowl combine water and cornstarch.
2. Mix it well, so no lumps remain.
3. Then add white sugar, coconut amino, vinegar, and garlic, ginger, and salt, pepper.
4. Mix it all well to combine well.
5. Coat chicken with the prepared marinade and let it sit for 30 minutes.
6. Preheat Ninja Foodi grill by pressing the "BAKE" at "350 degrees F" for 25 minutes.
7. Arrange the pan over the grill grate.
8. Once preheating is done add chicken pieces to the unit.
9. Bake it at high for 24 minutes.
10. Remember to flip halfway through.
11. Once done, serve.

Serving Suggestion: Serve with coleslaw and ranch

Variation Tip: Use soy sauce instead of coconut amino

Nutritional Information per Serving: Calories1035 | Fat 50.1g | Sodium 379mg | Carbs60 g | Fiber0.5g| Sugar 50.2g | Protein 95.4g

Orange and Honey Glazed Chicken

Prep: 16 Minutes | Cook Time: 15 Minutes | Makes: 2 Servings

Ingredients
- 4 garlic cloves, minced
- 1 teaspoon garlic powder
- 4 teaspoons onion powder
- ½ teaspoon pepper
- ½ cup teriyaki sauce
- ½ cup honey
- 1/3 cup orange marmalade
- 2 pounds chicken wings, bone-in

Directions
1. First, insert the grill grate in the ninja food grill and select the grill function.
2. Set the time to 15 minutes at medium.
3. Select start to begin preheating.
4. Meanwhile, in a large bowl mix the entire listed ingredient and let eh chicken wings marinade for 30 minutes.
5. Once preheating is done, add wings to the grill grate and cook for 15 minutes.
6. Remember to flip halfway through.
7. Serve and enjoy!

Serving Suggestion: Serve with ranch

Variation Tip: use maple syrup instead of honey

Nutritional Information per Serving: Calories 1349| Fat33.7g | Sodium3187 mg | Carbs 123.5g | Fiber 1.3g| Sugar 113.2g | Protein 137.3g

Alfredo Apple Chicken

Prep: Minutes | Cook Time: Minutes | Makes: Servings

Ingredients
- 1 tablespoon of apple juice
- 1 tablespoon lemon juice
- 4 chicken breasts, halved
- Salt and black pepper, to taste
- 4 teaspoons chicken seasoning
- ¼ cup blue cheese, crumbled

Directions
1. First, insert the grill grate in the ninja food grill and select the grill function.
2. Set the time to 20 minutes at medium.
3. Select start to begin preheating.
4. Meanwhile in a large mixing bowl and add chicken along with lemon juice, apple juice, salt, and black pepper.
5. Coat the chicken well with eh ingredients.
6. Once the unit beeps and preheating are done, arrange chicken over Grill Grate.
7. Lock the hood and then grill it at medium for 15 minutes.
8. Remember to flip halfway.
9. Once it's done serve it with sprinkle cheese on top.

Serving Suggestion: Serve with baked potatoes

Variation Tip: use Italian seasoning instead of poultry seasoning

Nutritional Information per Serving: Calories578 | Fat23 | Sodium 1652mg | Carbs16.6 g | Fiber 0.3g| Sugar 14.2g | Protein72 g

BBQ Chicken Thighs

Prep: 10 Minutes | Cook Time: 15 Minutes | Makes: 1 Serving

Ingredients

- 6 chicken thighs bone-in
- 1/3 cup barbecue sauce
- 2 tablespoons of peach preserve
- 2 tablespoons Lemon Juice
- Salt and black pepper, to taste

Directions

1. Take a bowl and start mixing barbecue sauce, peach preserve, salt, black pepper, and lemon juice.
2. Now trim the excess fat from the meat and place the chicken thighs in the marinade for 2 hours.
3. Now, preheat your Ninja Foodi Grill.
4. Once the unit beeps and preheating are done, arrange chicken over Grill Grate.
5. Lock the hood and then grill it at medium for 15 minutes.
6. Remember to flip halfway.
7. Once it's done serve hot.

Serving Suggestion: Serve it with coleslaw

Variation Tip: Use lime juice instead of lemon juice

Nutritional Information per Serving: Calories 444| Fat 16.4g | Sodium 600mg | Carbs 29.2g | Fiber 0.5 g| Sugar 20.5g | Protein 41.5 g

Grilled BBQ Chicken

Prep: 15minutes | Cook Time: 15 Minutes | Makes: 1 Serving

Ingredients

- 6 chicken thighs bone-in
- 2 tablespoons of Southwest Chipotle Seasoning
- 2 teaspoons of Garlic Powder
- 2 teaspoons of Onion Powder
- 1 teaspoon of Paprika
- 1 cup of BBQ sauce

Directions

1. Take a zip lock bag and add chicken thighs to it.
2. Then add seasoning, garlic powder, onion powder, paprika, and BBQ sauce and lock the zip lock bag
3. Set the zip lock bag aside for 20 minutes, so the chicken thighs get marinated.
4. Now, preheat your Ninja Foodi Grill.
5. Once the unit beeps and preheating are done, arrange chicken over Grill Grate.
6. Lock the hood and then grill it at medium for 15 minutes.
7. Remember to flip halfway
8. Once it's done serve hot.

Serving Suggestion: Serve it with Mac and cheese

Variation Tip: Use smoked paprika

Nutritional Information per Serving: Calories 1363| Fat 61.2g | Sodium 3092mg | Carbs 99.7g | Fiber3.1 g| Sugar68.2 g | Protein 96.6g

Yogurt Chicken Thighs

Prep: 15 Minutes | Cook Time: 25 Minutes | Makes: 3 Servings

Ingredients

- 1.5 pounds chicken thighs or legs
- 125 grams plain yogurt
- inch ginger, crushed
- 4-6 garlic cloves, crushed
- 1 teaspoon of red chili powder
- 2 tablespoons tandoori paste or powder
- 1 teaspoon turmeric
- 1 teaspoon coriander powder
- 1 teaspoon cumin powder
- 1 teaspoon Garam Masala
- Salt, to taste
- 1 tablespoon lemon juice
- 2 tablespoons of ghee

Directions

1. Combine all the listed ingredients in a large mixing bowl and rub the chicken with the marinade.
2. Let it sit for 30 minutes.
3. Arrange the crisper basket inside the unit.
4. Preheat Ninja Foodi grill by pressing the "BAKE" at "350 degrees F" for 25 minutes.
5. Once preheating is done add chicken pieces to the unit.
6. Bake it at high for 25 minutes.
7. Remember to flip halfway through.
8. Once done, serve and enjoy.

Serving Suggestion: Serve it with coleslaw or Mac and cheese

Variation Tip: Use olive oil instead of ghee

Nutritional Information per Serving: Calories 555| Fat 26.5g | Sodium336 mg | Carbs6.2 g | Fiber 0.6g| Sugar 3.2g | Protein68.7 g

Chicken Beans and Chili

Prep: 10 Minutes | Cook Time: 15 Minutes | Makes: 2 Servings

Ingredients

- 8 chicken breasts, cut into pieces
- 1 can corn
- ¼ teaspoon garlic powder
- 1 cup black beans, drained and rinsed
- 1 tablespoon canola oil
- 2 tablespoons chili powder
- 1 bell pepper, chopped
- ¼ teaspoon garlic powder
- ¼ teaspoon salt

Directions

1. The first step is to preheat the unit by pressing air crispy mode at 350 degrees F for 20 minutes.
2. Dump all the ingredients in the cooking basket.
3. Stir the ingredients once.
4. Let it air crisp at 390 degrees F for 15 minutes.
5. Once done, serve and enjoy.

Serving Suggestion: Serve it with salad

Variation Tip: Use olive oil instead of canola oil

Nutritional Information per Serving: Calories1146 | Fat26.9 g | Sodium 656mg | Carbs85.5 g | Fiber 20.2g| Sugar 8.2g | Protein 141g

Chicken Tomatina

Prep: 15 Minutes | Cook Time: 12 Minutes | Makes: 2 Servings

Ingredients
- 4 chicken breasts, Boneless and skinless
- ¼ cup fresh basil leaves
- 8 plum tomatoes
- 3/4 cup lemon juice
- 2 tablespoons olive oil
- 1 garlic clove, minced
- 1 –inch, ginger, chopped
- Salt and black pepper, to taste

Directions
1. Take a blender or a food processor and pulse together basil leaves, olive oil, salt, pepper, garlic and ginger, and lemon juice.
2. Then add the tomatoes and pulse them into a paste.
3. In a bowl add chicken and blended paste.
4. Let the chicken marinate in it for 30 minutes.
5. Now, pre-heat the unit for 15 minutes at 350 degrees F.
6. Now put the chicken inside the unit crisper basket.
7. Close the hood of the unit.
8. Lock the unit lid and let it cook for 12 minutes at AIR CRISP mode at 390 degrees F.
9. Remember to flip the chicken halfway through.
10. Once cooked, take out the chicken and serve.

Serving Suggestion: Serve with ranch

Variation Tip: Use canola oil instead of olive oil

Nutritional Information per Serving: Calories 545| Fat 20 g | Sodium 865mg | Carbs 27.9 g | Fiber 5.9g| Sugar 21.6 g | Protein 72 g

Snacks and Appetizers

Snack Time Pizza

Prep: 19 Minutes | Cook Time: 13 Minutes | Makes: 2 Servings

Ingredients

- 2 tablespoons all-purpose flour,
- Store-bought pizza dough (6 ounces)
- 1 tablespoon canola oil
- 1/2 cup pizza or Alfredo sauce
- 1 cup shredded mozzarella cheese
- 1/2 cup ricotta cheese
- 15 pepperoni slices

Directions

1. First, insert the grill grate in the ninja food grill and select the grill function.
2. Set the time to 25 minutes at medium.
3. Select start to begin preheating.
4. Roll out the pizza dough on a flat and clean work surface.
5. Keep adding flour to the dough so it does not stick.
6. Brush the surface of the dough with half of the canola oil
7. Poke the dough with a fork.
8. Once preheating is done, place dough on the grill grate.
9. Grill it for 5 minutes.
10. After 5 minutes take out the dough and layer sauce on it.
11. Then top it with the listed ingredients and drizzle canola oil on top.
12. Grill again for 3 minutes at medium.
13. Once done, serve hot.

Serving Suggestion: Serve with ranch

Variation Tip: Use olive oil instead of canola oil

Nutritional Information per Serving: Calories 1064| Fat 72g | Sodium 3695mg | Carbs 42.2g | Fiber 2.2g| Sugar3.2 g | Protein63.7 g

Air Crisp Chicken Tenders

Prep: 15 Minutes | Cook Time: 20 Minutes | Makes: 3 Servings

Ingredients
- 1.5 pounds of chicken tender
- Salt and black pepper, to taste
- 1 cup Panko bread crumbs
- 2 cups Italian bread crumbs
- 1-1/2 cup parmesan cheese
- 2 eggs
- Oil spray, for greasing
- 1 teaspoon of Italian seasoning

Directions
1. Rub the chicken tender with salt and black pepper.
2. Places Panko bread crumb in a bowl and add Italian bread crumb, parmesan cheese, and Italian seasoning to it.
3. Whisk eggs in a separate bowl.
4. Dip the chicken tender in eggs, then dredge the pieces in a crumb bowl and coat it very well.
5. Once the entire tenders are done, grease it with oil spray.
6. Preheat the unit by selecting AIR CRISP mode for 10 minutes at 375 degrees F.
7. Close the hood and start the unit.
8. Select START/PAUSE to begin the preheating process.
9. Once preheating is done, press START/PAUSE.
10. Once preheating is done add chicken pieces to the cooking basket of the unit.
11. Bake it at 375 for 20 minutes.
12. Remember to flip halfway through.
13. Once done, serve and enjoy.

Serving Suggestion: Serve it with ranch

Variation Tip: Use olive oil instead of oil spray

Nutritional Information per Serving: Calories 1095| Fat 38.2g | Sodium 2220mg | Carbs 81.2g | Fiber 4.3g| Sugar 8g | Protein 102.5g

Spicy Chicken Tenders

Prep: 12 Minutes | Cook Time: 20 Minutes | Makes: 2 Servings

Ingredients

- 2 large eggs, whisked
- 2 tablespoons lemon juice
- Salt and black pepper
- 1 pound of chicken tenders
- 2 cups Panko breadcrumbs
- 1 teaspoon smoked paprika
- 1/4 teaspoon garlic powder
- 1/4 teaspoon onion powder
- 1/2 cup fresh grated parmesan cheese

Directions

1. Preheat the unit by selecting AIR CRSIP mode for 10 minutes at 375degrees F.
2. Press the start to begin the preheating process.
3. Meanwhile, in a bowl whisk eggs and set them aside.
4. In a separate bowl mix lemon juice, smoked paprika, salt, black pepper, garlic powder, onion powder
5. In another bowl mix Panko breadcrumbs, and parmesan cheese.
6. Dredge the chicken tenders in the spice mixture then let it refrigerate for 10 minutes.
7. Next, dip each piece of chicken in the egg and then in a bread crumb mixture.
8. Once preheating is done add chicken pieces to the cooking basket of the unit.
9. AIR CRISPS it at 375 for 20 minutes.
10. Remember to flip halfway through.
11. Once done, serve and enjoy.

Serving Suggestion: Serve with ranch dressing

Variation Tip: None

Nutritional Information per Serving: Calories461 | Fat34.5 g | Sodium926 mg | Carbs18.8 g | Fiber 2.5g| Sugar 1.5g | Protein 92.5g

Grilled Watermelon

Prep: 15 Minutes | Cook Time: 2 Minutes | Makes: 2 Servings

Ingredients
- 6 watermelon slices, 3 inches across
- 2 tablespoons maple syrup

Directions
1. First, insert the grill grate in the ninja food grill and select the grill function.
2. Set the time to MAX for 3 minutes, by selecting grill function.
3. Select start to begin preheating.
4. Meanwhile, brush the watermelon slices with maple syrup on both the sides.
5. Once preheating is done, place the place watermelon on the grill grate.
6. Close the hood.
7. Grill it at MAX for 2 minutes.
8. Remember to flip it halfway through.
9. Once done, serve.

Serving Suggestion: Serve it with vanilla ice cream

Variation Tip: Use honey instead of maple syrup

Nutritional Information per Serving: Calories 310| Fat1.2 g | Sodium13 mg | Carbs77.9 g | Fiber 3.4g| Sugar64.6 g | Protein 5.1g

French Fries with Parmesan

Prep: 15 Minutes | Cook Time: 25 Minutes | Makes: 2 Servings

Ingredients

- 1 pound frozen French fries
- 1/3 cup mayonnaise
- 3 cloves garlic, minced
- 2 teaspoons garlic powder
- 1/4 teaspoon kosher salt
- 1/4 teaspoon ground black pepper
- A squeeze of lemon juice
- 2 tablespoons canola oil
- 1/3 cup grated Parmesan cheese
- 2 tablespoons parsley, chopped

Directions

1. First, put the crisper basket inside the unit and close the hood.
2. Select AIR CRISP mode at 350 degrees F for 20 minutes.
3. Select start to begin the preheating.
4. Once preheating is done, add frozen fries to the basket.
5. AIR crisps it at 375 degrees F for 25 minutes.
6. After 10 minutes, shake the basket.
7. And then close the hood and resume the cooking.
8. Meanwhile in a bowl combine garlic, mayonnaise, salt, garlic powder, pepper, and lemon juice
9. Once fries are done toss it in canola oil than in parmesan cheese and parsley.
10. Serve with mayo sauce.
11. Enjoy.

Serving Suggestion: Serve it with ketchup

Variation Tip: Use olive oil instead of canola oil

Nutritional Information per Serving: Calories 820| Fat 60g | Sodium 1498mg | Carbs 86.7g | Fiber8.6 g| Sugar5.3 g | Protein 22.7

Maple and Rosemary Chicken Wing

Prep: 15minutes | Cook Time: 23 Minutes | Makes: 4 Servings

Ingredients

- 1 tablespoon salt
- 1/2 teaspoon baking powder
- 1 teaspoon smoked paprika
- 2 pounds chicken wings, rinsed, patted dry
- 1 tablespoon garlic, minced
- 1 tablespoon lemon juice
- 1 teaspoon crushed red pepper
- 1 tablespoon fresh rosemary, chopped
- 1/4 cup Maple syrup

Directions

1. First, put the crisper basket inside the unit and close the hood.
2. Select AIR CRISP mode at 350 degrees F for 20 minutes.
3. Select start to begin the preheating.
4. As the unit is preheating, take a bowl and mix salt, baking powder, and smoked paprika rub the spice over the wings.
5. Once preheating is done add wings to the cooking basket of the unit.
6. AIR CRSIP for20minutes at 385degrees F.
7. As wings are cooking, take a bowl and combine lemon juice, garlic, red pepper, rosemary, and maple syrup
8. Remember to flip the chicken halfway through.
9. Once wings are cooked, transfer to the bowl of sauce and coat the wings.
10. Return the chicken to the basket and cook for 3 more minutes.
11. Once it's done serve.

Serving Suggestion: Serve with coleslaw

Variation Tip: use honey instead of maple syrup

Nutritional Information per Serving: Calories493 | Fat17.2 g | Sodium 1943mg | Carbs 15.4g | Fiber0.7 g| Sugar11.9 g | Protein 65.9g

Kale Chips

Prep: 15 Minutes | Cook Time: 8 Minutes | Makes: 2 Servings

Ingredients

- 2 cups spinach, torn in pieces and stem removed
- 2 cups kale, torn in pieces, stems removed
- 1 tablespoon of olive oil
- Sea salt, to taste
- 1/3 cup Parmesan cheese, grated

Directions

1. First, put the crisper basket inside the unit and close the hood.
2. Select AIR CRISP mode at 300 degrees F for 10 minutes.
3. Select start to begin the preheating.
4. Sprinkle salt over the spinach.
5. Then add olive oil to it.
6. Add kale and spinach to the crisper basket of the grill.
7. Select the air fry mode at 300 degrees F for 8 minutes.
8. Once done, take out the chips and sprinkle them with the Parmesan cheese.
9. Serve.

Serving Suggestion: Serve with chips

Variation Tip: None

Nutritional Information per Serving: Calories 217| Fat 15g | Sodium 508mg | Carbs9.4 g | Fiber 1.7g| Sugar 0.1g | Protein14.6 g

Stuffed Bell Peppers

Prep: 20 Minutes | Cook Time: 20 Minutes | Makes: 4 Servings

Ingredients

- 4 large bell peppers
- 1-1/2 cup rice, cooked
- 1 cup beef, cooked and minced
- 1 cup parmesan cheese
- 1 cup cheddar cheese, crumbled
- Salt and black pepper, to taste
- Oil spray, for greasing

Directions

1. Preheat the ninja air fryer grill by selecting AIR Crisp mode for 5 minutes at 375 degrees F.
2. Select START/PAUSE to begin the preheating process.
3. Meanwhile, cut the bell pepper lengthwise and remove any seed and center core the peppers
4. Mix the parmesan cheese, cheddar cheese, rice, and minced beef along with salt and pepper in a bowl and fill the cavity of bell pepper with it.
5. Grease the bell peppers with oil spray.
6. Once the unit is preheated add the bell peppers inside the unit in a crisper basket.
7. Set the time at 20 at 357 degrees at AIR CRISP mode.
8. Once it's done, serve.

Serving Suggestion: Serve with ranch

Variation Tip: None

Nutritional Information per Serving: Calories 1386| Fat 53.9g | Sodium 1310mg | Carbs 95.7g | Fiber 4.4g| Sugar 12.4g | Protein127.5 g

Cinnamon Butternut Squash

Prep: 15 Minutes | Cook Time: 12 Minutes | Makes: 2 Servings

Ingredients

- 1 tablespoon of sugar, powdered
- ½ teaspoon nutmeg
- 2 teaspoons cinnamon
- 2 tablespoons coconut oil
- 12 ounces butternut squash, fried-cut or cubed

Directions

1. Take a zip lock bag and add nutmeg, cinnamon, coconut oil, and sugar.
2. Add the butternut squash to it.
3. Toss and coat it and let it sit for 20 minutes.
4. Preheat the ninja air fryer grill by selecting AIR CRISP mode for 5 minutes at 375 degrees F.
5. Select START/PAUSE to begin the preheating process.
6. Insert the Crisper Basket, into the unit and add the butternut squash fries to the basket.
7. Select AIR CRISP, set the temperature to 400 degrees F, and set the time to 12 minutes.
8. Select START/STOP to start it completely.
9. Once cooked, and crispy serve and enjoy.

Serving Suggestion: Serve with fruits

Variation Tip: Use olive oil instead of coconut oil

Nutritional Information per Serving: Calories 225| Fat14 g | Sodium 7mg | Carbs 28g | Fiber4.7 g| Sugar10 g | Protein 1.8g

Stuffed Mushrooms

Prep: 10 Minutes | Cook Time: 8 Minutes | Makes: 2 Servings

Ingredients

- 2 cups Portobello mushrooms
- 2 tablespoons olive oil
- 1/2 cup ricotta cheese
- 6 tablespoons Parmesan cheese, divided
- 1 cup chopped spinach, thawed and drained
- 1 cup bread crumbs
- ¼ teaspoon rosemary, minced fresh

Directions

1. Preheat the ninja air fryer grill by selecting AIR CRISP mode for 3 minutes at 375 degrees F and close the hood.
2. Select START/PAUSE to begin the preheating process.
3. Coat the mushrooms with olive oil and remove the cap.
4. Bake mushrooms in the unit for 5 minutes.
5. Take a bowl and mix ricotta, Parmesan cheese, spinach, bread crumbs, and rosemary
6. Stuff this mixture into the mushroom caps.
7. Place the mushroom caps back into the unit crisper basket.
8. Bake for 3 minutes or until the filling is hot.
9. Enjoy.

Serving Suggestion: Serve it with ranch

Variation Tip: Use canola oil instead of olive oil

Nutritional Information per Serving: Calories 568| Fat 30.8g | Sodium 875mg | Carbs 45.2g | Fiber 2.3g| Sugar2.3 g | Protein 29.2g

Fried Broccoli

Prep: 12 Minutes | Cook Time: 10 Minutes | Makes: 2 Servings

Ingredients

- ¼ teaspoon of dry Masala
- ½ tablespoon red chili powder
- Salt, to taste
- ¼ tsp. turmeric powder
- 4 teaspoons of chickpea flour
- 4 teaspoons of plain yogurt
- 1 pound broccoli florets

Directions

1. Season the broccoli with salt and soak it in water for 1 hour.
2. Then take out the broccoli florets and drain.
3. Mix all remaining ingredients in a bowl and toss the broccoli in it
4. Insert the Crisper Basket in the unit.
5. Select AIR CRISP set the temperature to 390°F for 5 minutes.
6. Once the unit is preheated, add the marinated broccoli to the unit.
7. The air crisps it at 350°F, for 10 minutes and serve.

Serving Suggestion: Serve with cheese

Variation Tip: None

Nutritional Information per Serving: Calories 122| Fat 1.7g | Sodium 181mg | Carbs 22g | Fiber 8.1g| Sugar5.6 g | Protein8.8 g

Vegetables and Sides

Sweet Potato Fingers

Prep: 15 Minutes | Cook Time: 20 Minutes | Makes: 2 Servings

Ingredients
- 1 cup Panko breadcrumbs
- ½ teaspoon salt
- 1 pound sweet potatoes, peeled and sliced
- 250 ml of Aquafaba

Directions
1. Preheat the ninja Foodi grill by selecting AIR CRISP mode for 3 minutes at 375 degrees F and close the hood.
2. Select START/PAUSE to begin the preheating process.
3. In a mixing bowl, combine breadcrumbs and salt.
4. Coat the
5. Sweet potato slices first with the Aquafaba then put them in the breadcrumb mixture.
6. Place it inside the crisper basket, avoid overlapping.
7. Air Crisp for 20 minutes at 375degrees F.
8. Once done, serve and enjoy.

Serving Suggestion: Serve it with Ketchup

Variation Tip: None

Nutritional Information per Serving: Calories413 | Fat2.1 g | Sodium 1030mg | Carbs87.7 g | Fiber 16.3g| Sugar 2.3g | Protein 10.4g

Mexican Street Corn

Prep: Minutes | Cook Time: Minutes | Makes: 2 Servings

Ingredients
- 2 ears corn, shucked
- 1 tablespoon canola oil, divided
- Salt and black pepper, to taste

Sauce Ingredients
- 1 cup Cottage cheese, grated
- 1/4 cup mayonnaise
- 1/4 cup sour cream
- 1 lime, juiced
- ½ teaspoon garlic powder
- 1/2 teaspoon onion powder
- 1/8 cup fresh cilantro, chopped

Directions
1. Insert grill grate in the ninja Foodi grill.
2. Close the hood and preheat it at MAX for 10 minutes.
3. Meanwhile, brush the corn with canola oil and season it with salt and black pepper.
4. Once the unit is preheated grill the corn inside the unit for 7 minutes.
5. Afterward, flip the corns and then grill for 5 more minutes.
6. Meanwhile, mix all the sauce ingredients in a mixing bowl.
7. Once the corn is cooked serve it with sauce.

Serving Suggestion: Serve with shredded parmesan topping

Variation Tip: Use vegetable oil instead of canola oil

Nutritional Information per Serving: Calories 476| Fat 26.3g | Sodium 707mg | Carbs 42.2g | Fiber4.3 g| Sugar 7.7g | Protein 21.6g

Honey & Herb Charred Carrots

Prep: 10 Minutes | Cook Time: 6 Minutes | Makes: 2 Servings

Ingredients

- 2 teaspoons of honey
- 4 teaspoons of melted butter
- Salt, to taste
- 6 medium carrots
- 1 tablespoon of fresh parsley, chopped
- 1tablespoon of rosemary, chopped

Directions

1. First, insert the grill grate in the ninja Foodi grill and select the grill function
2. Set the time to MAX for 10 minutes, buy selecting grill function.
3. Select start to begin preheating.
4. Meanwhile in a small bowl add honey, salt, and melted butter.
5. Whisk the ingredients all well.
6. Coat the carrots with the honey butter and then rub with the listed herbs.
7. When the unit beeps and preheating is done, add the carrots to the cooking basket of the unit.
8. Close the hood and set it to MAX for 6 minutes at the grill mode.
9. Once done, serve.

Serving Suggestion: Serve with rice

Variation Tip: None

Nutritional Information per Serving: Calories 170| Fat 7.9g | Sodium260 mg | Carbs 25g | Fiber 5.3g| Sugar 14.8g | Protein 1.7g

Roasted Cauliflower

Prep: 20 Minutes | Cook Time: 10 Minutes | Makes: 2 Servings

Ingredients

- 1/2 head white cauliflower, cut in florets
- 1/2 head purple cauliflower, cut into florets
- 2 tablespoons extra virgin olive oil
- Salt and black pepper, to taste

Sauce Ingredients

- 2 tablespoons Asian chili paste
- 1/4 cup extra virgin olive oil
- 2 tablespoons rice wine vinegar
- 3 tablespoons maple syrup
- 1 tablespoon coconut amino
- 1/4 cup roasted peanuts
- 1tablespoon sesame seeds

Directions

1. Add the crisper basket in the ninja grill and close the hood.
2. Select the AIR CRISP mode and set the time to 25 minutes at 375 degrees F.
3. Next, take a bowl and combine cauliflower with oil, salt, and pepper.
4. Toss it to coat it finely.
5. Once the unit has preheated and timer beep adds the cauliflower to the basket.
6. Let it air crisp for 10 minutes.
7. Meanwhile, mix all sauce ingredients in a large mixing bowl.
8. Once cauliflower is done serve it with sauce.

Serving Suggestion: Serve it with rice

Variation Tip: None

Nutritional Information per Serving: Calories 534| Fat47 g | Sodium 40mg | Carbs 29.4g | Fiber 3.1g| Sugar 19.6g | Protein 6.5g

Grilled Tomato Salsa

Prep: 20 Minutes | Cook Time: 10 Minutes | Makes: 2 Servings

Ingredients

- 6 Roma tomatoes cut in half lengthwise
- ½ red onion, peeled, cut in quarters
- 2 jalapeño pepper, cut in half, seeds removed
- Salt and black pepper, to taste
- 2 tablespoons canola oil
- 1 bunch cilantro stems trimmed
- 3 cloves garlic, peeled
- 2 tablespoons ground cumin
- 1 teaspoon of lime zest
- 3 limes, juiced

Directions

1. Take a bowl and add onion, jalapeno, tomatoes, salt, canola oil, and black pepper.
2. Mix it very well.
3. First, insert the grill grate in the ninja food grill and select the grill function
4. Set the time to MAX for 10 minutes, buy selecting grill function.
5. Select start to begin preheating.
6. After the preheating is done, place the vegetable mixture from the bowl on the grill grate.
7. Close the hood and cook for 5 minutes.
8. After 5 minutes open the unit and flip the vegetables let it grill for 5 more minutes.
9. Once the grilling is one, transfer the ingredients from the unit to the food processor.
10. Add in the remaining listed ingredients as well, and pulse to form a salsa.
11. Once the salsa is prepared, serve and enjoy.

Serving Suggestion: serve with chips

Variation Tip: None

Nutritional Information per Serving: Calories 235| Fat 16.2g | Sodium 30mg | Carbs22.1 g | Fiber 6.3g| Sugar 11.6g | Protein5.1 g

Eggplant with Greek yogurt

Prep: 18 Minutes | Cook Time: 10 Minutes | Makes: 1 Serving

Ingredients
- 1 large eggplant, sliced
- 2 tablespoons olive oil
- 1 cup Greek yogurt
- 1 teaspoon sweet paprika
- Salt and black pepper, to taste
- 1 lime cut in half

Directions
1. Season the eggplant with salt and let it sit for 30 minutes to remove the bitterness.
2. Wash and pat dry the eggplants.
3. First, insert the grill grate in the ninja food grill and select the grill function.
4. Set the time to MAX for 10 minutes, buy selecting grill function.
5. Select start to begin preheating.
6. Season the eggplants with paprika, pepper, oil add lime juice.
7. Once preheating is done, add the eggplants to the Grill Grate and close the hood.
8. Select the GRILL function and set the temperature to the MAX setting.
9. Let it grill for 8-10 minutes.
10. Once done, serve the eggplants with a dollop of Greek yogurt.

Serving Suggestion: Serve over rice

Variation Tip: Use plain yogurt as an alternative

Nutritional Information per Serving: Calories 1288| Fat 53.4g | Sodium 404mg | Carbs83 g | Fiber19 g| Sugar 63.5g | Protein 126.6g

Stuffed Jalapeno

Prep: 15 Minutes | Cook Time: 5 Minutes | Makes: 1 Serving

Ingredients

- 2 eggs, whisked
- 1 cup cottage cheese
- 1 cup almond flour
- 4 jalapenos, cut lengthwise and seeds removed
- ¼ teaspoon of garlic powder
- ¼ teaspoon onion powder
- ¼ teaspoon of Cajun seasoning
- Black pepper and salt, to taste

Directions

1. Put the Crisper Basket inside the unit.
2. Then close the hood.
3. Select AIR CRISP, at 400 degrees F, for 5 minutes.
4. Select the start to begin preheating.
5. Mix all dry spice ingredients in a bowl.
6. Whisk eggs in another bowl.
7. Fill the cavity of jalapeño with cheese, and then dip it in egg wash then coat it with flour mixture.
8. Add the jalapenos to the Air Crisper basket ad grease it with oil spray.
9. Air crisp at 350 degrees F, for 5 minutes.
10. Once done, serve.

Serving Suggestion: Serve it with ketchup

Variation Tip: Use any other cheese variation you liked

Nutritional Information per Serving: Calories517 | Fat 28g | Sodium 2425mg | Carbs 20g | Fiber5.4 g| Sugar 4.7g | Protein 50g

Parmesan, Cheddar, And Zucchini Casserole

Prep: 20 Minutes | Cook Time: 30 Minutes | Makes: 4 Servings

Ingredients

- 1 egg, whisked
- 6 saltine crackers, or as needed, crushed
- 3 tablespoons bread crumbs
- 1 pound yellow squash, sliced
- 1pound zucchini, sliced
- ½ cup Cheddar cheese
- ½ cup of parmesan cheese
- ½ onion, diced
- ½ cup biscuit baking mix
- 1/2 cup butter
- Oil spray, for greasing

Directions

1. Take a crisper basket and grease it with oil spray, and place it inside the ninja Foodi grill.
2. Select AIR CRISP mode and set it to 10 minutes at 350 degrees F.
3. Let the preheating begin.
4. Take a bowl and add zucchini, yellow squash, and onion and add it to the crisper basket once preheating is done.
5. Cook it for 15 minutes, at 360° F, or until tender.
6. Take a bowl and whisk eggs in it along with butter, baking mix, parmesan, and cheddar cheese.
7. Pour it over vegetables in a basket and then top it with cracker and bread crumbs.
8. Let it air crisp for 15 minutes at 390 degrees F.
9. Once done, serve and enjoy.

Serving Suggestion: Serve with salad

Variation Tip: None

Nutritional Information per Serving: Calories 513| Fat 38.2g | Sodium 989mg | Carbs 23.5g | Fiber 2.9g| Sugar6.2 g | Protein17.8 g

Artichokes with Honey Dijon

Prep: 15 Minutes | Cook Time: 15 Minutes | Makes: 2 Servings

Ingredients

- 6 whole artichokes
- ½ gallon water
- Sea salt to taste
- ¼ cup raw honey
- ¼ cup boiling water
- 3 tablespoons of Dijon mustard

Directions

1. Cut the artichokes lengthwise in half.
2. Simmer artichokes in water and salt mixture for 20 minutes.
3. First, insert the grill grate in the ninja food grill and select the grill function.
4. Set the time to MAX for 8 minutes, buy selecting grill function.
5. Select start to begin preheating.
6. Remove the artichokes from the water.
7. Pat dry and then drizzle it with olive oil and salt.
8. Once the unit is preheated grill artichokes by placing them on the grill grate for 15 minutes at MAX.
9. Remember to flip the artichokes halfway through.
10. Mix the honey, boiled water, and Dijon in a bowl.
11. Baste the artichokes with the mixture until they absorb the mixture.
12. Once done, serve and enjoy.

Serving Suggestion: Serve it with cheese dip

Variation Tip: None

Nutritional Information per Serving: Calories 145| Fat 0.9g | Sodium 416mg | Carbs 36.5g | Fiber 1g| Sugar 35g | Protein 1.3g

Garlic and Sage Tomatoes

Prep: 10Minutes | Cook Time: 6 Minutes | Makes: 2Servings

Ingredients
- ½ tablespoon sage, chopped
- 6 plum tomatoes
- 1 tablespoon of olive oil
- Salt and black pepper, to taste
- 1 cup feta cheese, sliced

Directions
1. Cut the tomatoes in half and then season them with salt, black pepper, and olive oil.
2. Press the sage leaves in the center of the tomatoes.
3. First, insert the grill grate in the ninja food grill and select the grill function.
4. Set the time to MAX for 8 minutes, buy selecting grill function.
5. Select start to begin preheating.
6. Once prehearing is done, arrange the tomato inside the unit onto grill grates.
7. Grill 4 to 6 minutes at MAX.
8. Remember to flip halfway through.
9. Once done, serve with feta cheese slices.

Serving Suggestion: Serve it with baked potato or salad

Variation Tip: None

Nutritional Information per Serving: Calories 345| Fat 23.5g | Sodium 885mg | Carbs22.2 g | Fiber4.3 g| Sugar17.8 g | Protein 15.2g

Fish and Seafood

Teriyaki Salmon

Prep: 15 Minutes | Cook Time: 8 Minutes | Makes: 4 Servings

Ingredients
- 4 salmon fillets (6 ounces each), uncooked
- 1 cup teriyaki marinade
- Oil spray, for greasing

Directions
1. Marinate the fish fillets in the teriyaki sauce for 1 hour in the refrigerator.
2. Meanwhile, insert the grill grate in the ninja food grill and select the grill function.
3. Remember to grease the grill grate with oil spray.
4. Set the time to MAX for 10 minutes, buy selecting grill function.
5. Select start to begin preheating.
6. Once the timer beeps add fillets to the grill grate and cook for 6 minutes at MAX.
7. If the desired doneness is not achieved let it grill for 2 more minutes.
8. Then serve and enjoy hot.

Serving Suggestion: serve with rice

Variation Tip: None

Nutritional Information per Serving:
Calories349 | Fat12.4 g | Sodium1028 mg | Carbs 22.5g | Fiber 0g| Sugar 20g | Protein37 g

Grilled Citrusy Halibut

Prep: 15 Minutes | Cook Time: 10 Minutes | Makes: 4 Servings

Ingredients

- 1 teaspoon of lemon zest
- 2 tablespoons of lemon juice
- Salt and black pepper, to Taste
- ½ teaspoon ginger, minced
- 1 teaspoon garlic, minced
- 4 tablespoons canola oil
- 2tablespoons parsley, minced
- 2 tablespoons maple syrup
- 2 halibut fillets (6 ounces each)

Directions

1. First, insert the grill grate in the ninja food grill and select the grill function.
2. Remember to grease the grill grate with oil spray.
3. Set the time to MAX for 12 minutes, buy selecting grill function.
4. Select start to begin preheating.
5. Take a bowl and combine all the listed ingredients in it excluding fish.
6. Then spoon the marinade on top of the fish and let it sit for 20 minutes.
7. Once the ninja a Foodi grill timer beeps add the fillet to the grill grate.
8. Pour any extra sauce on top of fish.
9. Let the fish grill for 10 minutes at MAX.
10. Once done, serve.

Serving Suggestion: Serve with chips

Variation Tip: none

Nutritional Information per Serving: Calories 314| Fat 17.5g | Sodium 82mg | Carbs 7.5g | Fiber 0.2g| Sugar 6.2g | Protein30.4 g

Salmon with Herbs

Prep: 15 Minutes | Cook Time: 12 Minutes | Makes: 2 Servings

Ingredients
- 2 lemons, juice only
- 1/3 cup fresh mint, chopped
- ¼ cup fresh parsley, chopped
- 1 tablespoon Dijon mustard
- 1 garlic clove
- Salt and black pepper, to taste
- 1 pound center-cut salmon, skinned

Directions
1. Combine all the listed ingredients excluding fish in a blender and process.
2. Add a few tablespoons of water if needed.
3. Once the smooth paste is formed, marinate fish in it for 30 minutes.
4. Next, insert the grill grate in the ninja food grill and select the grill function.
5. Remember to grease the grill grate with oil spray.
6. Set the time to MAX for 8 minutes, buy selecting grill function.
7. Select start to begin preheating.
8. Once done with the preheating adds fillets to the grill and close the hood.
9. GRILL at MAX, for 12 minutes.
10. Flipping is not necessary.
11. Once cooked, serve the fish.

Serving Suggestion: Serve it with salad or ranch

Variation Tip: Use yellow mustard instead of Dijon.

Nutritional Information per Serving: Calories 637| Fat 20| Sodium 433mg | Carbs2.7 g | Fiber 1.6g| Sugar0.2 g | Protein105 g

Lemon Pepper Shrimp

Prep: 12 Minutes | Cook Time: 8 Minutes | Makes: 1 Serving

Ingredients

- 10 large Shrimps
- 2 tablespoons of Vegetable oil, avocado
- 1 tablespoon of Lemon pepper seasoning.

Directions

1. Coat the shrimp with vegetable oil and lemon pepper seasoning
2. Rub it all well.
3. Next, insert the grill grate in the ninja food grill and select the grill function.
4. Remember to grease the grill grate with oil spray.
5. Set the time to MAX for 8 minutes, buy selecting grill function.
6. Select start to begin preheating.
7. Once the unit is preheated add the fish to the grill grate and close the hood
8. Grill at MAX for 8 minutes.
9. Flipping the shrimp is not necessary.
10. Once done, serve.

Serving Suggestion: Serve with rice

Variation Tip: None

Nutritional Information per Serving: Calories 263| Fat 16g| Sodium 270mg | Carbs3.7 g | Fiber 0.9g| Sugar 0g | Protein 25.4g

Glazed Salmon

Prep: 15 Minutes | Cook Time: 10 Minutes | Makes: 2 Servings

Ingredients

- ½ tablespoon of lemon pepper
- 1 /2 tablespoon everything bagel seasoning
- Salt, pinch
- 1teasoon old bay seasoning
- 2 tablespoons of butter
- 2 salmon fillets, 8 ounces each
- 1 tablespoon honey

Directions

1. Insert the grill grate in the ninja food grill and select the grill function.
2. Remember to grease the grill grate with oil spray.
3. Set the time to MAX for 8 minutes, buy selecting grill function.
4. Select start to begin preheating.
5. Take a bowl and mix honey with melted butter, old bay seasoning, salt, bagel seasoning, and lemon pepper.
6. Mix well and coat the fish with the glaze evenly.
7. Once coated, wait for the unit to get preheated
8. One beef sounds, add the fillets to the grill grate and close the hood.
9. Grill at max for 8 minutes.
10. Once done, serve and enjoy.

Serving Suggestion: Serve it with baked potato

Variation Tip: Use olive oil instead of butter

Nutritional Information per Serving: Calories373 | Fat22.6g | Sodium239 mg | Carbs 9.7g | Fiber0.4 g| Sugar8.6g | Protein 34.9

Smoked Shrimp

Prep: 15 Minutes | Cook Time: 7Minutes | Makes: 1 Serving

Ingredients

- 10 large shrimps
- 1 teaspoon smoked paprika
- 1 teaspoon thyme, dry
- Salt, pinch
- ¼ teaspoon garlic powder
- ¼ onion powder
- ½ teaspoon cayenne pepper
- ¼ teaspoon of lemon zest

Directions

1. Insert the grill grate in the ninja food grill and select the grill function.
2. Remember to grease the grill grate with oil spray.
3. Set the time to MAX for 8 minutes, buy selecting grill function.
4. Select start to begin preheating.
5. Mix the entire rub and spices in a bowl and then coat the shrimp with the spice rub.
6. Spray the shrimp with oil spray and transfer to the grill grate.
7. Let it grill at MAX for 7 minutes.
8. Flipping is not necessary.
9. Once it's done, serve.

Serving Suggestion: Serve with cheese dip

Variation Tip: None

Nutritional Information per Serving: Calories 80| Fat 1.4g| Sodium291 mg | Carbs 3.8g | Fiber1.5 g| Sugar 0.5g | Protein13.2 g

Salmon with Creamy Lime Sauce

Prep: 20Minutes | Cook Time: 8 Minutes | Makes: 2 Servings

Ingredients

Sauce Ingredients

- 1 tablespoon lime zest, grated
- 4 teaspoons brown sugar
- Salt, to taste
- 1/3 cup lime juice
- 4 tablespoons olive oil
- 2 tablespoons white wine vinegar
- 1/3 teaspoon coriander
- 1/3 cup chopped fresh cilantro
- 1 tablespoon finely chopped onion
- 1 tablespoon of chopped tomatoes
- 2 cups Greek yogurt

Salmon Ingredients

- 1 tablespoon olive oil
- 1/4 teaspoon salt
- 1/4 cup minced fresh ginger root
- 2 tablespoon lime juice
- 1/4 teaspoon freshly ground pepper
- 4 salmon fillets (6 ounces each)
- Oil spray, for greasing

Directions

1. Take a bowl and combine all the listed sauce ingredients.
2. Mix it well and set it aside for further use.
3. Now take a separate bowl and add salt, lime juice, pepper, and olive oil .
4. Rub the fish fillet with the mixture.
5. Grease the fillets with oil spray.
6. Insert the grill grate in the ninja food grill and select the grill function.
7. Remember to grease the grill grate with oil spray.
8. Set the time to MAX for 8 minutes, buy selecting grill function.
9. Select start to begin preheating.
10. Once done with preheating add fillets in batches into the grill and let it cook at MAX for 8 minutes, per batch.
11. Once done, serve hot with sauce.

Serving Suggestion: Serve with Rice

Variation Tip: Use canola oil or butter instead of olive oil

Nutritional Information per Serving: Calories1330 | Fat 62g| Sodium473 mg | Carbs 28.6g | Fiber0.3g| Sugar 27.5g | Protein 164.5g

Salmon with Cream Cheese

Prep: 15 Minutes | Cook Time: 8 Minutes | Makes: 2 Servings

Ingredients

- 4 salmon fillets, 6 ounces each
- 6 ounces cream cheese
- 2 tablespoons mayonnaise
- 2 teaspoons of parsley, chopped
- 2 teaspoon of lemon juice
- Salt and black pepper
- Oil spray, for greasing

Directions

1. Cut the salmon fillet into small pieces and season it with salt, black pepper, and grease it with oil spray.
2. Insert the grill grate in the ninja food grill and select the grill function.
3. Remember to grease the grill grate with oil spray.
4. Set the time to MAX for 8 minutes, buy selecting grill function.
5. Select start to begin preheating.
6. Once beeps sound add salmon to the grill and grill it at MAX for 8 minutes.
7. Meanwhile, take a bowl and combine parsley, lemon zest, salt, mayonnaise, cream cheese in a bowl.
8. Serve the cooked fillet with creamy sauce and enjoy.

Serving Suggestion: Serve with rice

Variation Tip: None

Nutritional Information per Serving: Calories829 | Fat 56.9g| Sodium 515mg | Carbs6 g | Fiber 0.1g| Sugar1.2 g | Protein 75.5g

Sea Food Omelet

Prep: 12 Minutes | Cook Time: 6 Minutes | Makes: 1 Serving

Ingredient

- 10 large shrimp, shells removed and chopped
- 4 eggs, beaten
- 1/3 cup of black olives, chopped
- 1 pinch paprika
- Salt and black pepper, to taste
- Oil spray, for greasing
- 2 tablespoons of coconut milk

Directions

1. Crack eggs in a bowl and pour in the coconut milk.
2. Whisk both the ingredients well
3. Now add black olives, salt, paprika, and pepper to the eggs.
4. Mix well and add shrimp.
5. Take a small cake pan and grease it with oil spray.
6. Pour the egg mixture inside it and top it with diced shrimp.
7. Add the cake pan to the crisper basket and insert it to the unit.
8. Press AIR CRISP function and let it cook for 6 minutes, at 375 degrees F.
9. Once done, sprinkle cheese on top and let it air crisp for 2 more minutes.
10. Serve it hot.

Serving Suggestion: Serve it with bread slices

Variation Tip: Use green olives instead of black olives

Nutritional Information per Serving: Calories 640| Fat 33.8| Sodium1179 mg | Carbs 9.4g | Fiber2.2 g| Sugar2.4 g | Protein 73.4g

Shrimp Poppers

Prep: 12 Minutes | Cook Time: 7 Minutes | Makes: 2 Servings

Ingredients
- 1 lb shrimp (455 g), deveined and peeled

Seasoned Flour
- 1 cup flour (125 g)
- 1 tablespoon Cajun seasoning
- 2 teaspoons salt
- 1 teaspoon black pepper

EGG MIXTURE Ingredients
- 1 egg
- 3 tablespoons milk
- 1 teaspoon Cajun seasoning

Directions
1. Take a small bowl and whisk the egg in it then add Cajun seasoning and milk to the egg mixture.
2. Whisk it well and set it aside for further use.
3. In a separate bowl mix together Cajun seasoning, salt, pepper, and flour.
4. Set it aside as well.
5. Now dip the shrimp first in egg wash then in flour mixture.
6. Once all the shrimps are coated let it sit in the refrigerator for 20 minutes.
7. Add the crisper basket and insert it into the unit.
8. Press AIR CRISP function and let it preheat for 10 minutes at 375 degrees F.
9. Then grease the crisper plate with oil spray.
10. Add the coated shrimp to the basket and let it air crisp at 375 degrees F for 7 minutes.
11. Once all the shrimps are done, serve.

Serving Suggestion: Serve with ranch

Variation Tip: Use almond flour instead of plain flour

Nutritional Information per Serving: Calories 543 | Fat 7.1g| Sodium 2997mg | Carbs 53.1g | Fiber 2g| Sugar 1.4g | Protein 62g

Pineapple Fish Fillet

Prep: 15 Minutes | Cook Time: 7 Minutes | Makes: 2 Servings

Ingredients

- 1 teaspoon of Chili powder as needed
- 1/ 2 cup cilantro leaves, chopped
- 1 tablespoon lime juice
- Salt and black pepper to taste
- ½ tablespoon canola oil
- 2 fillet salmon, 6-8 ounces
- 2 tablespoons of pineapple juice, fresh squeezed
- 1 cup grilled pineapple slices

Directions

1. Take a blender and pulse cilantro with canola oil.
2. Add salt and black pepper.
3. Then add the lime juice, chili powder, and pineapple juice.
4. Now rub the fillet with the blended mixture.
5. Pre-heat your Ninja Foodi Grill to MAX set a timer to 12 minutes.
6. Once preheating done, grill the fillets and grill for 7 minutes.
7. Once done serve it with grilled pineapple.

Serving Suggestion: Serve it with coleslaw

Variation Tip: Use olive oil instead of canola oil

Nutritional Information per Serving: Calories 320 | Fat 14.3 | Sodium 115mg | Carbs 4.8 g | Fiber 0.9g| Sugar 3.7g | Protein 44.5g

Coconut Battered Fish Fillets

Prep: 15 Minutes | Cook Time: 10 Minutes | Makes: 2 Servings

Ingredients

- Salt and pepper to taste
- ½ teaspoon mustard powder
- 2 teaspoons of garlic powder
- 1/3 cup plain flour
- 1 cup coconut flour
- Oil spray, for greasing
- 2 fish fillets, salmon (6 ounces each)

Directions

1. Insert the grill grate in the ninja food grill and select the grill function.
2. Remember to grease the grill grate with oil spray.
3. Set the time to MAX for 8 minutes, buy selecting grill function.
4. Select start to begin preheating.
5. Meanwhile, mix salt, pepper, mustard powder, garlic powder, and coconut flour in a bowl.
6. Season the fish with salt and black pepper and coat it with oil spray.
7. Once the unit is preheated add the fish to the grill grate and grill at MAX for 10 minutes
8. No needed to flip the fillets.
9. Once it's done serve.

Serving Suggestion: Serve it with rice

Variation Tip: Use almond flour and plain flour

Nutritional Information per Serving: Calories333 | Fat 12.9g| Sodium500 mg | Carbs 37.7g | Fiber 3.9g| Sugar 1.3g | Protein17.2g

Beef, Pork, And Lamb

Ninja Foodi Grill Steak and Potatoes

Prep: 18 Minutes | Cook Time: 27 Minutes | Makes: 2 Servings

Ingredients

- 4 potatoes russet
- 2 sirloin steaks
- 1/4 cup avocado oil
- 2 tablespoons steak seasoning
- Sea salt, to taste

Directions

1. Wash, peel, and pat dry the potatoes.
2. Coat the potatoes with avocado oil and season them with salt and black pepper.
3. Preheat the ninja Foodi grill by putting it to air crisp mode for 20 minutes at375 degrees F.
4. Once predated add potatoes to the crisper basket and the air crisp for 15minutes at 400degrees F.
5. Season the steak with salt and black pepper.
6. Take out the crisper basket from the unit and adjust the grill grate.
7. Grill the steak at MAX for 12 minutes.
8. Flip it halfway through.
9. Once done, serve the steak with air fry potatoes.

Serving Suggestion: Serve with ranch

Variation Tip: use canola oil instead of avocado oil

Nutritional Information per Serving: Calories 1817| Fat44.3 g | Sodium 722mg | Carbs 129.3g | Fiber15 g| Sugar6.6 g | Protein 216.1g

Ninja Foodi Grill Steak

Prep: 15 Minutes | Cook Time: 12 Minutes | Makes: 1 Serving

Ingredients

- 1 Rib eye steak
- Salt and pepper, to taste
- 2 tablespoons of steak seasoning
- Oil spray, for greasing

Directions

1. Season the steak with steak seasoning, salt, and pepper.
2. Insert the grill grate in the ninja food grill and select the grill function.
3. Remember to grease the grill grate with oil spray.
4. Set the time to MAX for 8 minutes, buy selecting grill function.
5. Select start to begin preheating.
6. Once preheating done, spray the steak with oil spray.
7. Add the steak to the grill grate and cook for 12 minutes at MAX.
8. Flip halfway through.
9. Once done, serve and enjoy.

Serving Suggestion: Serve over rice or baked potatoes

Variation Tip: use olive oil instead of oil spray

Nutritional Information per Serving: Calories 699| Fat52.6 g | Sodium 152mg | Carbs 0.1g | Fiber0 g| Sugar 0g | Protein53.2 g

Grilled Steak

Prep: 20 Minutes | Cook Time: 12 Minutes | Makes: 1 Serving

Ingredients

- 1 New York steak, 8 ounces
- 2 tablespoons of vegetable oil
- 2 teaspoons of steak seasoning
- Salt and black pepper, to taste

Directions

1. Insert the grill grate in the ninja food grill and select the grill function.
2. Remember to grease the grill grate with oil spray.
3. Set the time to MAX for 8 minutes, buy selecting grill function.
4. Select start to begin preheating.
5. Whisk the vegetable oil with seasoning, salt, and black pepper.
6. Brush the steak with seasoning.
7. Once preheating is done, add it to the unit grill grate grill at MAX for 12 minutes once done, serve and enjoy.

Serving Suggestion: Serve it with coleslaw

Variation Tip: use olive oil instead of vegetable oil

Nutritional Information per Serving: Calories 508| Fat 27.2g | Sodium3069 mg | Carbs66.8 g | Fiber 0g| Sugar 53.4g | Protein 0g

Soy Pork Ribs

Prep: 20 Minutes | Cook Time: 17 Minutes | Makes: 2 Servings

Ingredients

- 1 pound pork ribs
- ¼ cup balsamic vinegar
- ½ cup of soy sauce
- 1 teaspoon garlic powder
- ¼ cup hoisin sauce
- Salt, pinch

Directions

1. In a large bowl mix the entire ingredient and marinate the ribs in it for 3 hours by placing the refrigerator.
2. Turn on the unit and press Grill at "MED" and set the timer to 25 minutes.
3. Once the timer beeps, transfer the marinated pork ribs to the grill grates.
4. Cook for 17 minutes at MAX.
5. Flip halfway through.
6. Then serve hot.

Serving Suggestion: Serve with rice

Variation Tip: None

Nutritional Information per Serving: Calories 734| Fat 41.3g | Sodium 4321mg | Carbs20.3 g | Fiber 1.6g| Sugar 10.3g | Protein 65.5g

Lamb Chops

Prep: 15 Minutes | Cook Time: 15 Minutes | Makes: 2 Servings

Ingredients

- ½ tablespoon Dijon mustard
- 1 cup honey, packed
- ¾ cup bourbon
- ½ cup hot sauce
- 1 cup ketchup
- 4 tablespoons Worcestershire sauce
- ¼ cup of soy sauce
- Salt and pepper to taste
- 8 boneless pork chops

Directions

1. Insert grill grate inside the unit and preheat it by setting it to "MAX" mode.
2. Set the timer to 15 minutes.
3. Once preheating is done, transfer the Lamb chops to grill grates.
4. Cook for 12 minutes at MAX, flip halfway through.
5. In a saucepan add the remaining ingredients and simmer at medium heat.
6. Once the boil comes, lower the heat and drizzle the sauce over grilled pork chops.
7. Serve hot and enjoy.

Serving Suggestion: Serve with mashed potato

Variation Tip: Use hot sauce instead of ketchup

Nutritional Information per Serving: Calories1760 | Fat 52g | Sodium 6798mg | Carbs 184g | Fiber 1.3g| Sugar 172g | Protein 105g

Air Fry Ground Beef

Prep: 15 Minutes | Cook Time: 15 Minutes | Makes: 2 Servings

Ingredients
- 1 pound ground beef, not frozen
- Salt and black pepper, to taste
- 1 teaspoon of dry taco seasoning

Directions
1. Preheat the air fryer by inserting a crisper basket in it.
2. Let it set to 350 degrees F for 15 minutes at AIR CRISP mode.
3. Add it to the crisper basket.
4. Set it to AIR CRISP mode at 10 minutes.
5. Rub-dry taco seasoning, salt, and black pepper onto the meat and add it to the crisper basket.
6. Set it to AIR CRISP mode at 375 degrees F, for15 minutes.
7. Once cooked, take out the groined meat and serve.

Serving Suggestion: Serve with pasta

Variation Tip: None

Nutritional Information per Serving: Calories 421| Fat14.1 g | Sodium 150mg | Carbs0 g | Fiber 0g| Sugar 0g | Protein 69g

Beef Jerky

Prep: 20 Minutes | Cook Time: 5 Hours Minutes | Makes: 4 Servings

Ingredients

- 2 pounds beef roast, sliced thinly
- 1 tablespoon of jerky mix

Directions

1. Cut the beef into strips
2. Remove any silver skin.
3. Season beef roast with jerk mix.
4. Store it in the fridge for 4 hours.
5. Add the beef to the crisper basket and set it to dehydrate for 5hours at 150 degrees F.
6. Once done, serve and enjoy.

Serving Suggestion: Serve with eggs

Variation Tip: None

Nutritional Information per Serving: Calories421 | Fat 14.1g | Sodium 150mg | Carbs 0g | Fiber 0g| Sugar0 g | Protein69 g

Pork Chops

Prep: 30 Minutes | Cook Time: 23 Minutes | Makes: 2 Servings

Ingredients

- 6 pork chops
- ½ teaspoon garlic powder
- ½ teaspoon onion salt
- 1 teaspoon parsley
- ½ teaspoon thyme
- ½ teaspoon basil
- Salt and black pepper, to taste
- 2 tablespoons olive oil

Directions

1. Insert the grill grate in the ninja food grill and select the grill function.
2. Remember to grease the grill grate with oil spray.
3. Set the time to MAX for 12 minutes, buy selecting grill function.
4. Select start to begin preheating.
5. Take a blender and blend olive oil, salt, pepper, garlic powder, onion salt, parsley, thyme, and basil.
6. Rub this paste all over the pork chops.
7. Once preheating is done, transfer the Lamb chops to grill grates.
8. Cook for 23 minutes at MEDIUM, flip halfway through.
9. Once cooked, take out and serve hot.

Serving Suggestion: Serve with rice

Variation Tip: Use canola oil instead of olive oil

Nutritional Information per Serving: Calories891 | Fat 73.3g | Sodium449 mg | Carbs0.8 g | Fiber0.2 g| Sugar0.2 g | Protein 54.1g

Sausages in Ninja Grill

Prep: 20 Minutes | Cook Time: 15 Minutes | Makes: 2 Servings

Ingredients

- 4 beef sausages
- 2 bell peppers, whole
- 1 onion, sliced
- Oil spray, for greasing

Directions

1. Preheat the ninja grill by selecting air crisp.
2. Mode for 5 minutes at 325 degrees F.
3. Select start/pause to begin the preheating.
4. Afterward add the sliced bell pepper, sliced onions, and sausage to a crisper basket of unit
5. Drizzle olive oil, salt, and pepper over vegetables.
6. Lock the hood.
7. Set it to grill mode at low for 15 minutes.
8. Remember to flip the ingredients halfway through.
9. Once it's done and serve.

Serving Suggestion: Enjoy with baked beans

Variation Tip: None

Nutritional Information per Serving: Calories 165| Fat 10.1g | Sodium 215mg | Carbs 15g | Fiber 2.8 g| Sugar 8.3g | Protein 5.4g

Greek Yogurt Lamb Chops

Prep: 20 Minutes | Cook Time: 17 Minutes | Makes: 2 Servings

Ingredients

- 1 cup Greek yogurt
- 2 lemons, juice only
- 1 teaspoon cumin, ground
- 1 teaspoon coriander, ground
- ¼ teaspoon Italian seasoning
- Salt and black pepper, to taste
- 6 rib lamb chops, ¼ inches thick cut
- 2 tablespoons olive oil, divided

Directions

1. Combine Greek yogurt, lemon juice, cumin, coriander, Italian seasoning, salt, pepper, and olive oil.
2. Marinate the lamb chops in the marinade for2 hours.
3. Insert the crisper basket in the unit and preheat it for 20 minutes at 350 degrees F.
4. Once preheating is done grease the basket with oil sprays and adds lamb chops to the basket.
5. AIR CRIPS at 375 degrees F for 17 minutes.
6. Once done, serve and enjoy.

Serving Suggestion: Serve with coleslaw

Variation Tip: Use plain yogurt instead of Greek yogurt

Nutritional Information per Serving: Calories 730| Fat 95.4g | Sodium 451mg | Carbs28.8 g | Fiber0.1 g| Sugar28.3 g | Protein 132.2g

Steak & Vegetable Kebabs

Prep: 15 Minutes | Cook Time: 8 Minutes | Makes: 4 Servings

Ingredients

- 2 New York strip steaks (10–12 ounces each), cut into cubes
- 10 white button mushrooms, cut in half, stems removed
- 1 bell pepper cut into 2-inch pieces
- 2 white onions, peeled, cut in quarters, petals cut in 2-inch pieces
- Salt, as desired
- Ground black pepper, as desired
- Steak seasoning, as needed
- Oil spray, for greasing

Directions

1. Insert the grill grate in the ninja food grill and select the grill function.
2. Remember to grease the grill grate with oil spray.
3. Set the time to MAX for 8 minutes, buy selecting grill function.
4. Select start to begin preheating.
5. Meanwhile, assemble the skewers by layering them with mushroom, steak, bell pepper, and onion, down to the end of the skewers.
6. Season it with salt, black pepper, steak seasoning, and drizzle olive oil on top.
7. Once preheating is done place skewers on the grill grate.
8. Grill at MAX for 8 minutes without flipping.
9. Once done, serve.

Serving Suggestion: Serve with ranch

Variation Tip: None

Nutritional Information per Serving: Calories 410| Fat16.8 | Sodium 148mg | Carbs 8.9g | Fiber 2g| Sugar 4.6g | Protein 53.9g

Lamb Chops with Coconut

Prep: 20 Minutes | Cook Time: 23 Minutes | Makes: 3 Servings

Ingredients

- Oil spray, for greasing
- 6 lamb chops
- Salt and ground black pepper, to taste
- 2 tablespoons butter, for frying
- 1 tablespoon red curry paste
- 1 cup of coconut cream
- 4 tablespoons fresh cilantro, grated
- 2 green chilies, grated

Directions

1. Mix salt, pepper, butter, red curry paste, cilantro, green chilies, and coconut cream
2. Mix it all well and rub it all over the lamb chops.
3. Refrigerate the lamb chops for 3 hours.
4. Next, Insert the grill grate in the ninja food grill and select the grill function.
5. Remember to grease the grill grate with oil spray.
6. Set the time to MAX for 8 minutes, buy selecting grill function.
7. Select start to begin preheating.
8. Once preheating is done, transfer the Lamb chops to grill grates.
9. Cook for 23 minutes at MEDIUM, flip halfway through.
10. Once cooked, take out and serve hot.

Serving Suggestion: Serve with rice

Variation Tip: Use olive oil instead of butter

Nutritional Information per Serving: Calories 794| Fat 58.5g| Sodium 327mg | Carbs 15.5g | Fiber 1.8g| Sugar 2.7g | Protein 51.9g

Rosemary Lamb Chops

Prep: 12 Minutes | Cook Time: 7 Minutes | Makes: 2 Servings

Ingredients
- 4 Lamb Chops
- 2 teaspoons of Olive Oil
- 1 teaspoon of rosemary
- 1teaspoon of Garlic
- 2 tablespoons of Garlic Puree
- Salt & Pepper, to taste

Directions
1. Insert the grill grate in the ninja food grill and select the grill function.
2. Remember to grease the grill grate with oil spray.
3. Set the time to MAX for 8 minutes, buy selecting grill function.
4. Select start to begin preheating.
5. Once preheating is done add lamb chops to the bowl and finely brush it with olive oil, salt, and black pepper, and minced garlic.
6. Top it with a fresh spring of rosemary and unpeeled garlic let it marinate in the refrigerator for 20 minutes.
7. Once preheating is done, add lamb to the grill grate with the remaining ingredients grill it for 7 minutes at MAX.
8. Remember to flip halfway through.
9. Once done, serve.

Serving Suggestion: Serve with salad

Variation Tip: Use canola oil instead of olive oil

Nutritional Information per Serving: Calories1128 | Fat 70g | Sodium 1mg | Carbs 21.8g | Fiber 0.6g| Sugar0g | Protein 100.3g

Best Pork Chops

Prep: 15 Minutes | Cook Time: 22 Minutes | Makes: 2 Servings

Ingredients

- 4 bone-in pork chops, 2 inches thick
- 2 tablespoons brown sugar
- 2 tablespoons paprika
- 1 teaspoon yellow mustard
- ½ teaspoon onion powder
- ¼ teaspoon garlic powder
- 4 tablespoons olive oil
- Salt, to taste

Directions

1. Preheat the air fryer at 400 degrees for 10 minutes by pressing AIR CRISP mode.
2. Meanwhile, rinse and pat dry the pork chops.
3. Add all the listed ingredients it the bowl and rub the pork with the spices.
4. Marinate it for 1 hour
5. Once preheating is done.
6. Add the pork chop to the crisper basket and lock the hood.
7. Set a timer to 22 minutes at 375 degrees in an air crisp mode, flipping pork chops over after 6 minutes.
8. Once done, serve and enjoy.

Serving Suggestion: Serve with rice

Variation Tip: Use butter instead of olive oil.

Nutritional Information per Serving: Calories 779| Fat53 g | Sodium 1531mg | Carbs 15.5g | Fiber2.7 g| Sugar11.8 g | Protein 60g

Dessert

Banana and Chocolate Chip Pudding

Prep: 15 Minutes | Cook Time: 22 Minutes | Makes: 4 Servings

Ingredients:
For Bread Pudding
- 12 ounces bread, cubed
- 1 cup banana, peeled, cored, and chopped
- ½ cup chocolate chips
- ¼ cup walnuts, chopped
- 2 cups milk
- ¾ cup water
- 6 tablespoons honey
- 1 teaspoon ground cinnamon
- 2 teaspoons cornstarch
- 2 teaspoons vanilla extract

Ingredients for Topping
- 1 1/2 cups plain flour
- ¼ cup brown sugar
- 6 tablespoons butter

Directions
1. Take a large bowl and combine bread slices, bananas, walnuts, chocolate chips in it.
2. In a separate bowl, add the remaining listed ingredients under pudding ingredients mix until well combined.
3. Pour this milk mixture on top of the bread mixture and let the bread absorb some of the liquid
4. Refrigerate for about 20 minutes.
5. Now, mix all the topping ingredients in it.
6. Pour the topping over the refrigerated bread mixture.
7. Arrange the "Crisper Basket" inside the Ninja Foodi Grill.
8. Close the Ninja Foodi Grill with lid and select "Air Crisp".
9. Set the temperature to 375 degrees F for 15 minutes
10. Press start to begin the preheating.
11. Afterward, place the bread pan into the "Crisper Basket".
12. Set the time for 22 minutes at AIR CRISP mode.
13. Once done, serve.

Serving Suggestion: Serve it with ice-cream
Variation Tip: None
Nutritional Information per Serving: Calories947 | Fat34 g | Sodium783 mg | Carbs143 g | Fiber5.9 g| Sugar 59.8g | Protein 19.5g

Lava Cake

Prep: 10 Minutes | Cook Time: 8 Minutes | Makes: 3 Servings

Ingredients

- 2/3 cup chocolate chips
- ½ cup unsalted butter
- 2 large eggs
- 2 large egg yolks
- 1 cup confectioners' sugar
- 1/3 cup all-purpose flour plus more for dusting

Directions

1. Melt butter and chocolate chips by placing them in a microwave using a microwave-safe bowl.
2. In a separate bowl whisk eggs and egg yolk, and add sugar and beat until well combined.
3. Then dump in the chocolate and the flour and stir to combine.
4. Grease 3 large-sized ramekins and dust with some flour.
5. Pour the mixture into the prepared ramekins.
6. Arrange the "Crisper Basket" in the Ninja Foodi Grill.
7. Select "Air Crisp" and set the temperature to 375 degrees F to preheat for 20 minutes.
8. When the display shows "Add Food" opens the hood
9. Place the ramekins into the "Crisper Basket".
10. Let it AIR CRISP for 8 minutes.
11. Once cooked, serve and enjoy after it gets cool off.

Serving Suggestion: Serve it with vanilla Ice-cream

Variation Tip: Use brown sugar as a sugar alternative.

Nutritional Information per Serving: Calories816 | Fat50 g | Sodium 300mg | Carbs92 g | Fiber 1.3g| Sugar 86.2g | Protein9.5 g

Delicious Pie

Prep: 10 Minutes | Cook Time: 22 Minutes | Makes: 2 Servings

Ingredients

- ¾ cup brown sugar
- ¼ cup caster sugar
- 1/3 cup butter, melted
- 2 large eggs
- 1¾ tablespoons flour
- 4 tablespoons milk
- 1 teaspoon vanilla extract
- 1 cup pecan halves
- 1 frozen pie crust, thawed

Directions

1. Whisk butter with sugar and then add whisked eggs, and combine all the ingredients well.
2. Then pour in the milk and add the remaining listed ingredients excluding pie crust.
3. Whisk it all well.
4. Arrange the crust in an oil greased pie pan.
5. Pour the bowl mixture over the crust.
6. Put the "Crisper Basket" in the unit.
7. Set the temperature to 320 degrees F to preheat at AIRCRISP mode.
8. Once preheating is done, put the pie pan in the unit.
9. Close the hood and set the timer for 22 minutes.
10. Once cooking is complete, serve and enjoy.

Serving Suggestion: Serve it with fresh cream

Variation Tip: Use almond milk instead of dairy milk

Nutritional Information per Serving: Calories 1519| Fat106.5 g | Sodium 729mg | Carbs 131.5g | Fiber8.5 g| Sugar 85.2g | Protein20 g

Chocolate Chip Cake

Prep: 15 Minutes | Cook Time: 18 Minutes | Makes: 2 Servings

Ingredients

- Salt, pinch
- 2 eggs, whisked
- ½ cup brown sugar
- ½ cup butter, melted
- 10 tablespoons of almond milk
- ¼ teaspoon of vanilla extract
- ½ teaspoon of baking powder
- 1 cup all-purpose flour
- 1 cup of chocolate chips
- ½ cup of cocoa powder

Directions

1. Whisk the egg in the bowl and add all the wet ingredients to it.
2. Take a separate bowl and mix all the dry ingredients.
3. Now combine both the ingredients bowl.
4. Pour this batter into the round baking pan.
5. Put it inside the basket of the unit.
6. Set the time to 18 minutes at 350 degrees F at AIR FRY mode.
7. Once done, serve.

Serving Suggestion: Serve with coffee

Variation Tip: use coconut milk instead of almond milk

Nutritional Information per Serving: Calories 1507| Fat 96.6g | Sodium 560mg | Carbs 150.1g | Fiber12.6 g| Sugar81.9 g | Protein24.6 g

Blueberry Muffins

Prep: 20 Minutes | Cook Time: 18 Minutes | Makes: 2 Servings

Ingredients

- ½ cups of all-purpose flour
- 1 teaspoon baking powder
- 2 large eggs
- Salt, pinch
- 3/4 cup white sugar
- 1/2 cup dark brown sugar
- 1 cup blueberry
- 1/4 cup almond milk

Directions

1. Take 4 ramekins and grease them with oil spray.
2. Take a bowl and whisk the egg in it.
3. Add white and brown sugar to eggs and whisk well.
4. Then add the baking powder, and salt, and pour in the milk.
5. Add in all-purpose flour and stir all the ingredients well.
6. At the end folds in the blueberries.
7. Pour this batter into 4 ramekins.
8. Now, put the ramekins inside the crisper basket and close the hood.
9. Set the time to 18 minutes at 360 degrees Fat AIR CRISP mode.
10. Once done, serve and enjoy.

Serving Suggestion: Serve it with Vanilla ice-cream

Variation Tip: Use Coconut milk instead of almond milk

Nutritional Information per Serving: Calories891 | Fat13 g | Sodium166 mg | Carbs172 g | Fiber 4.2g| Sugar118.2 g | Protein14 g

Bread Pudding

Prep: 15 Minutes | Cook Time: 14 Minutes | Makes: 3 Servings

Ingredients

- Oil spray, for greasing ramekins
- 3 slices of white bread, crumbled
- 6 tablespoons of white sugar
- 6 large eggs
- ½ cup cream
- Salt, pinch

Directions

1. In a bowl whisk eggs and add white sugar.
2. Whisk it well and then add cream and salt.
3. Add in the white bread pieces to the ramekins.
4. Pour the egg batter over the greased ramekins.
5. Put it inside the ninja air fryer crisper basket.
6. Set it to AIR CRISP mode at 14 minutes.
7. Once done, serve and enjoy.

Serving Suggestion: Serve it with coffee

Variation Tip: None

Nutritional Information per Serving: Calories284 | Fat12.7 g | Sodium 265mg | Carbs 30.6g | Fiber0.2 g| Sugar 26g | Protein3.6 g

Vanilla Cake

Prep: 15 Minutes | Cook Time: 30 Minutes | Makes: 2 Servings

Ingredients

- 90 grams all-purpose flour
- Pinch of salt
- 1/2 teaspoon of baking powder
- 2 eggs
- 1 teaspoon of vanilla extract
- 10 tablespoons of white sugar

Directions

1. Take a bowl and add all-purpose flour, salt, and baking powder.
2. Stir it in a large bowl.
3. Whisk two eggs in a separate bowl and add vanilla extract, sugar and blend it with a hand beater.
4. Now combine wet ingredients with the dry ones.
5. Mix it well and pour it into a round pan that fits inside the basket.
6. Place the pan inside the basket.
7. Now set it to BAKE function at 310 for 30 minutes.
8. Once it's done, serve and enjoy.

Serving Suggestion: Serve with coffee

Variation Tip: Use baking soda instead of baking powder

Nutritional Information per Serving: Calories459 | Fat 459g | Sodium 141mg | Carbs95.5 g | Fiber 1.3g| Sugar60.7 g | Protein 10.2g

Grilled Pineapple

Prep: 10 Minutes | Cook Time: 10 Minutes | Makes: 2 Servings

Ingredients

- 2 cups pineapple, sliced

Directions

1. Insert the grill grate in the ninja food grill and select the grill function.
2. Remember to grease the grill grate with oil spray.
3. Set the time to MAX for 8 minutes, buy selecting grill function.
4. Select start to begin preheating.
5. Once the preheating is done, add the pineapple to the grill grate.
6. Grill it at MAX for 10 minutes.
7. Flip several times during cooking.
8. Once done serve with whipping cream.

Serving Suggestion: Serve with ranch

Variation Tip: None

Nutritional Information per Serving: Calories60 | Fat 0g | Sodium10 mg | Carbs 15g | Fiber 1g| Sugar 13g | Protein 0g

Grilled Cinnamon Apple

Prep: 15 Minutes | Cook Time: 7 Minutes | Makes: 2 Servings

Ingredients
- 4 small firm apples, cored
- 2 tablespoons brown sugar
- ½ teaspoon cinnamon
- Salt, pinch

Directions
1. Slice the apple and sprinkle it with brown sugar, a pinch of salt, and cinnamon.
2. Insert the grill grate in the ninja food grill and select the grill function.
3. Remember to grease the grill grate with oil spray.
4. Set the time to MAX for 8 minutes, buy selecting grill function.
5. Select start to begin preheating.
6. Once the preheating is done, add the apple slices to the grill grate.
7. Grill it at MAX for 7 minutes.
8. Flip several times during cooking.
9. Once done serve and enjoy.

Serving Suggestion: Serve it with cream

Variation Tip: None

Nutritional Information per Serving: Calories268 | Fat 0.8 | Sodium 84mg | Carbs 71g | Fiber11.1 g| Sugar 55.1g | Protein1.2 g

Grilled Bananas

Prep: 10 Minutes | Cook Time: 3 Minutes | Makes: 2 Servings

Ingredients

- 6 bananas, sliced, Peel, cut in half lengthwise
- 1 tablespoon cinnamon
- Salt, pinch

Directions

1. Insert the grill grate in the ninja food grill and select the grill function.
2. Remember to grease the grill grate with oil spray.
3. Set the time to MAX for 8 minutes, buy selecting grill function.
4. Select start to begin preheating.
5. Drizzle cinnamon and salt over the bananas.
6. Once the preheating is done, add the banana slices to the grill grate.
7. Grill it at MAX for 3 minutes.
8. Flipping halfway through.
9. Once grilled, remove it using silicone-tipped tongs.
10. Enjoy.

Serving Suggestion: Serve it with fresh whipped cream

Variation Tip: None

Nutritional Information per Serving: Calories323 | Fat1.2 g | Sodium 83.6mg | Carbs 83.2g | Fiber11 g| Sugar43.4 g | Protein4 g

30 Days Meal Plan

Days	Breakfast	Lunch	Dinner
Day 1	Spinach Omelet	Ninja Foodi Grill Savory Chicken Breast	Yogurt Chicken Thighs
Day 2	Mushroom And Black Olives Omelet	Chicken With Tzatziki Sauce	Lamb Chops
Day 3	Spinach And Cheese Muffins	Lamb Chops	Salmon With Creamy Lime Sauce
Day 4	Regular Grilled Cheese Bread	Steak & Vegetable Kebabs	Lamb Chops With Coconut
Day 5	Sea Food Omelet	Cheesy Chicken Wings	Glazed Salmon
Day 6	Spinach And Cheese Muffins	Crispy Chicken	Ninja Foodi Grill Savory Chicken Breast
Day 7	Spinach Omelet	Alfredo Apple Chicken	Lamb Chops
Day 8	Spinach And Cheese Muffins	Grilled BBQ Chicken	Cheesy Chicken Wings
Day 9	Breakfast Hash	Ninja Foodi Grill Savory Chicken Breast	Honey Garlic Chicken Wings
Day 10	Spinach Omelet	Ninja Foodi Grill Savory Chicken Breast	Orange And Honey Glazed Chicken
Day 11	Breakfast Soufflé	Maple And Rosemary Chicken Wing	Eggplant With Greek Yogurt
Day 12	Sea Food Omelet	Ninja Foodi Grill Steak And Potatoes	
Day 13	Breakfast Hash	Air Crisp Drumstick	Grilled Citrusy Halibut
Day 14	Regular Grilled Cheese Bread	Ninja Foodi Grill Savory Chicken Breast	Best Pork Chops
Day 15	Breakfast Soufflé	Soy Pork Ribs	Yogurt Chicken Thighs
Day 16	Banana And Chocolate Chip Pudding	Ninja Foodi Grill Steak And Potatoes	Cheesy Chicken Wings

Day			
Day 17	Sea Food Omelet	Rosemary Lamb Chops	Grilled Bbq Chicken
Day 18	Spinach Omelet	Ninja Foodi Grill Savory Chicken Breast	Grilled Citrusy Halibut
Day 19	Breakfast Soufflé	Honey Garlic Chicken Wings	Best Pork Chops
Day 20	Sourdough Sandwich	Maple And Rosemary Chicken Wing	Glazed Salmon
Day 21	Air Fry Sweet Potatoes	Salmon With Herbs	Smoked Shrimp
Day 22	Banana And Chocolate Chip Pudding	Orange And Honey Glazed Chicken	Stuffed Mushrooms
Day 23	Mushroom And Black Olives Omelet	Coconut Battered Fish Fillets	Salmon With Creamy Lime Sauce
Day 24	Breakfast Hash	Bbq Chicken Thighs	Lamb Chops With Coconut
Day 25	Sausages In Ninja Grill	Grilled Chicken	Glazed Salmon
Day 26	Regular Grilled Cheese Bread	Teriyaki Salmon	Grilled Steak
Day 27	Sausages In Ninja Grill	Lamb Chops With Coconut	Salmon With Cream Cheese
Day 28	Mushroom And Black Olives Omelet	Salmon With Creamy Lime Sauce	Pineapple Fish Fillet
Day 29	Breakfast Hash	Grilled Steak	Orange And Honey Glazed Chicken
Day 30	Spinach Omelet	Salmon With Creamy Lime Sauce	Salmon With Herbs

Conclusion

All the myths are gone now, as the Ninja Foodi grill is one of the best appliances that help you prepare food using an outdoor grill, but with less hustle.

Its capacity allows you to prepare family meals with its simple touch functions and buttons.

No doubt the other brands cannot compete it hand-free cooking experience. All of its preset modes and instructions are easy to follow. Once you buy this appliance you will be impressed by its astonishing results.

Printed in Great Britain
by Amazon